SATTVA

SATTVA

7 steps to achieve clarity, purpose & balance in your life

Graeme E. Duncan

TORCHLIGHT
PUBLISHING

Copyright © 2013 Graeme E. Duncan

All rights reserved. No part of this book may be reproduced, stored in a retrieval system or transmitted in any form, by any means, including mechanical, electronic, photocopying, recording, or otherwise, without the prior written consent of the author.

Printed in the United States of America

Book design: Yamaraja Dasa
Cover photos:
Stepping stones ©iStockphoto.com / Felix Möckel
Sunrise ©iStockphoto.com / Elena Petrova

Library of Congress Cataloging-in-Publication Data

Duncan, Graeme E., 1966–
　Sattva : seven steps to achieve clarity, purpose and balance in your life / by Graeme E. Duncan.—1st Edition.
　　pages cm
　Includes bibliographical references.
　ISBN 978-1-937731-02-1
　1. Self-actualization (Psychology) 2. Cognitive balance.
　3. Well-being—Religious aspects—Vaishnavism. I. Title.
　BF637.S4D8596 2013
　158—dc23
　　　　　　　　　2012043692

Contents

Acknowledgments *xi*
Foreword *xiii*
Introduction *xv*

CHAPTER 1
My Personal Story 1
   Learning to Ride the Machine Called "Education" 2
   Taking Off the Training Wheels 3
   Life's Valuable Lessons 5
   Empowered Relationships 5
   Sattva Clarity Found 6
   Abundance 7
   Search for Mastery 7
   A Quick Recap 9

CHAPTER 2
The Secret Power of Sattva 11
   A Lifetime of Searching 11
   Sattva Defined 13
   Balance Is the Key 15
   Tapping Our Psychic Energy 16
   Understanding the Mind 17
   Who Are the Happiest People in the World? 18
   External Influences on Our Consciousness 19
   Sattva: Life in Perfect Balance 20
   A Quick Recap 22

CHAPTER 3
Principle 1: The Triangle of Health   23

    The Diet/Health Disconnect   24

    Stuck Between the Media and the Healthcare System   25

    The High Cost of Our Low-Cost Foods   26

    One Example: High-Fructose Corn Syrup (HFCS)   26

    Bisphenol-A: The Resin in the Lining of Tin Cans   27

    Another Example: High Cholesterol   28

    A Healthy Diet: The Real Solution   29

    Quick Nutrition 101   30

    An Inconvenient Truth: Diet and the Environment   33

    Physical Fitness and Exercise   36

    Top Twenty Advantages of Exercise   38

    The Effects of Stress—Baboons and Civil Servants   40

    Mothers Aging Six Times Faster   42

    Solutions to Stress   43

    Meditation and Breathing   44

    Music As a Tool for Transformation and De-Stressing   48

    A Quick Recap   51

CHAPTER 4
Principle 2: Finding Your Purpose   53

    Loss of Purpose   53

    Your Intrinsic Identity and Purpose   54

    Great Minds Think Alike   55

    Discovering Your Dharma   56

    A Guided Meditation for Vocational Clarity   58

    Discovering Opportunities in Life   61

    Pay Attention—Ask Questions   62

    Beware of Your Own "Opportunity Damper"   64

    Discretion, the Better Part of Valor   66

Balancing Internal and External Goals   67
The Process for Fulfilling External Goals   67
The Process of Making Internal Changes   68
Happiness and Purpose   69
Four Reasons Successful People Are Happy   71
A Quick Recap   71

CHAPTER 5
Principle 3: Empowering Your Relationships   73

Finding the Right Starting Point   73
Elusive Love   74
Obstacles on the Path of Love   76
Up Your Love Ante   77
Resolving Relationship Issues   78
Relationships and Responsibility   80
Generating a Vibration of Love   81
Learning How to Resonate Love   82
The Five Varieties of Loving Relationships   83
The Progression of Relationships   84
Creating a Peaceful Space   86
Attentive and Effective Communication   87
Errors in Communication   87
Jumping the Gun   88
Mirroring for Clarity   89
Communicating to Empower Others   89
A Quick Recap   90

CHAPTER 6
Principle 4: Sattva Clarity—Removing Inner Roadblocks   93

Dispelling Negative Core Beliefs   93

Real-Life Examples   94
Changing Behavior to Strengthen New Patterns   99
Ignoring the Mind   102
Constant Improvement: The RASIC System   103
Asking the Right Questions   103
Releasing Self-Judgment   104
The Two Sources of Self-Judgment   104
Concentrate on the Present   106
Positive Steps You Can Take   106
The Most Devestating of All Emotions   108
Ending the Tendency to Criticize   109
Protect Your Positive State of Mind   110
Overcoming Your "Immunity to Change"   112
Adaptive Thinking Versus Linear Thinking   113
The Strength of Faulty Assumptions   118
Striving to Consume or Improve?   120
A Quick Recap   121

CHAPTER 7
Principle 5: Abundance Mindset   123
Think in Terms of Abundance   123
Nurturing and Weeding   125
Abundance and Opening Your Heart   126
People, Not Things, Bring True Happiness   128
Universal Abundance   129
A Quick Recap   131

CHAPTER 8
Principle 6: Being in the Present   133
The "Bliss" of High-Risk Behavior   133
Looking in the Wrong Places   134

Getting into the "Zone" or Sattva   136
Understanding the Flow of Consciousness   137
Wasteful Mental Chatter   140
Arriving at Presence   140
Connecting to the Present   143
Harness the Mind with Intelligence   144
Happiness: The Result of Being "Present"   145
Unconditional Happiness Blocked   148
The Trap of Consumerism   149
Beliefs that Lock Out Happiness   150
The Law of Diminishing Returns   150
Pleasure and Pain Come of Their Own Accord   152
Summary of Steps to Uncovering
    Your Internal Happiness   153
A Quick Recap   154

CHAPTER 9
Principle 7: Sattva Mastery   157

The First Step to Living the Life of Your Dreams   157
What Is Mastery?   159
Enjoying the Pursuit of Mastery   159
Type B and Type M Persons   160
The Culture of Steady Improvement   162
Transforming Your Emotional State   164
Max Linder on Influencing Others   168
Build Your Will Power   168
Empower Your Decisions   170
Generating Enthusiasm   170
Consciousness and the Power of Focus   171
Harnessing the Power of Focus   172
Focus for Peak Performance   173

    Selective Perception   175
    The Three Waves in the Ocean of Emotions   177
    Understanding the Waves of Life to Unlock Their Power   178
    Riding the Right Wave   181
    A Quick Recap   183

CHAPTER 10
Sattva and Faith   185
    Self-Improvement in Wisdom Literature   186
    Improvement Begins from the Core   188
    Look Within First   189
    A Quick Recap   190

CHAPTER 11
Balancing a Society
On the Verge of Change   191
    Mounting Dissatisfaction   192
    Striving for Idealism   195
    The Balance of Wisdom and Compassion   196
    Empathy and Wisdom   196
    A Quick Recap   198

CONCLUSION
What's Next?   199

    Glossary   201
    List of Works Cited   205

Acknowledgments

I thank all those wonderful people who are too numerous to list here, who have inspired me in my life to improve and upgrade my consciousness. I would also like to thank David Bridges and Dr. Deborah Klein for helping me with the editing of this work, my wife and two daughters for encouraging me to complete it, and Percy Garcia who encouraged me to write it in the first place. And thanks to all the wonderful people at Torchlight for their expertise and professionalism.

Graeme E. Duncan
November 22, 2012
Thanksgiving Day

> *"Not what we say about our blessings,*
> *but how we use them,*
> *is the true measure of our thanksgiving."*
> —W. T. Purkiser

Foreword

THIS BOOK OFFERS READERS a successfully harvested crop of Eastern as well as Western wisdom, especially drawing from the body of wisdom coming from sacred India.

As the voices of spiritual wisdom do, our author, Graeme Duncan, focuses on the quality of life. Elevation to a higher awareness, a greater pursuit of life, a more effective pursuit of one's personal life goals, is the thrust of the work. A reading of these pages will transmit to us select aspects of this wisdom and its practical application for contemporary life. And in places in this book, the author also draws from his own experience and life journey, with its challenges and successes, offering us windows into his own life from which we can learn.

The thread that runs throughout this book is the notion of *sattva*. A literal translation could be "beingness" or "trueness," pointing us to "awareness," "clarity," or "authenticity." To discover greater meaning, purpose, and authentic activity in life is the journey on which the author desires to take us.

The word *sattva* also indicates the human capacity for greater acceptance of the joys and sorrows that life brings. It is what is often commonly referred to as a "reality check." It is about learning "to see things as they are." To develop a greater sensitivity to ourselves and others and life itself, to develop an ability to put things in perspective, with greater focus, with greater appreciation, is quite a challenge, and our author provides concrete suggestions for achieving this.

I urge readers to take the journey, to live a life filled with the clarity of *sattva*—a life that shows, in exhilarating ways, how to reach those things and find those things of which you had previously only dreamed, but now that you can put into focus, realize, and have.

>   —Graham M. Schweig, Ph.D.,
>   University Professor,
>   teacher of classical yoga,
>   author of *Dance of Divine Love*,
>   (Princeton University Press, 2005)

Introduction

HUMANITY HAS ENDEAVORED for progress and improvement since antiquity. Individually, we find ourselves in a ready-made world where great strides in technology and science have shaped our lives to be easier and more comfortable. This culture of modern convenience, however, has proven to be inadequate in fulfilling our desire to achieve personal satisfaction, happiness, purpose and mastery. It's becoming more and more obvious that we need to rethink the direction we are going in individually and collectively as a society and a planet.

I have made it my habit to inquire about the realizations of people from all walks of life. These pearls of wisdom hint toward universal truths. It is such truths that find their confluence in ancient writings and traditions where timeless secrets have been hidden. Unlocking these ancient jewels and codifying them into simple principles has drastically changed the quality and depth of my experience. Countless people throughout the ages have attained success and mastery by following these seven principles. I am not concocting anything new, just sharing my realizations and making these universal principles easy to understand and apply in day-to-day life.

What makes this book different from other self-help books is that it helps the reader connect to the core of the self within. It is when we come in contact with the essence of our being, that our relationships, interactions and existence in this world become more vibrant, meaningful, and successful. Uncovering the layers to our inner self is like removing unnecessary heavy baggage carried throughout life. When we learn to center our consciousness within our real self, we discover that even things we thought very difficult are now achieved with great ease. The practical steps to uncovering those layers are systematically outlined in this book and our seminars. The process renews our energy levels at each stage. This book is dedicated to those individuals who strive to unlock their greatness and full potential and are searching for the most organic way to do so.

An important lesson, and the thread upon which the seven principles in this book are strung, is that consciousness is the most valuable asset we possess. Consciousness, when recognized as our internal power source which can be charged or depleted, is called psychic energy. By understanding how to accumulate the power of consciousness and avoid the depletion of our conscious energy, we begin to understand *sattva*—our true inherent nature. If we neglect to elevate and upgrade our key asset of consciousness, life becomes stagnant.

Sattva is another interwoven thread found throughout the book. *Sattva* is the center of gravity of consciousness, or the fulcrum where we balance consciousness. By discovering the power of *sattva* we learn how to become happy, successful, and achieve mastery through pursuing our purpose in life. *Sattva* is the most efficient resting place for consciousness. By understanding and balancing our consciousness in *sattva* we discover the balance in everything. With this deep understanding we can remove even great obstacles and achieve our cherished goals through leverage. By using the tools in this book, we move our life toward lasting success, happiness, and mastery.

The ancient *Veda*s of India have been a great source of inspiration to this work, especially the knowledge locked in the *Upanishad*s and *Purana*s. The extraordinary translations and commen-

Introduction

taries on ancient Puranic writings by A. C. Bhaktivedanta Swami Prabhupada have revealed him to be a titan among transcendentalists of devotion. The crystallized gems of realization in such writings enrich the heart and nourish the soul.

The chapters in this book can be read independently and referred to periodically as you progress toward living life at a higher resolution. The knowledge in these pages can be applied by anyone no matter their age or situation in life. I have kept the writing simple so that it may be easy to grasp the fundamental concepts. The first two chapters offer an introduction as well as my personal story. From chapter three to nine the seven principles are described, and chapters ten and eleven offer some concluding thoughts. This book was written following the course material for our seminars and workshops.

A lot of ground is covered, as it offers the serious enquirer full access to principles that transform and enhance life. Even if someone gleans one realization from any of the principles, I will consider this effort a success.

CHAPTER 1
My Personal Story

*"I know of no more encouraging fact
than the unquestionable ability of man to elevate
his life by conscious endeavor."*
—Henry David Thoreau

SHORTLY AFTER my birth, my parents went through a lengthy divorce. Since my mother was unemployed at the time, she had no means to support her children. My father was working but he refused to support his children. Due to these circumstances my three siblings and I became wards of the state and were sent to Nazareth House, a Catholic orphanage. The orphanage, which was situated at the foot of Table Mountain in Cape Town, South Africa, had large grounds that included a chapel, a nunnery, an orphanage for the older children, a nursery for the very young children, tennis courts, and a swimming pool. It was nestled among extensive grounds with pine tree forests and manicured flower beds. Since I was only two years old, I was separated from my siblings and placed in the nursery.

At Nazareth House, one of my earliest memories of altered consciousness occurred when I was a toddler, sitting in front of an alcove containing a statue of Mother Mary, reciting the Holy Rosary. One of the nuns in the nursery, Sister Patrick, had taken the time to teach me how to recite the Rosary, and made sure that every day I spent at least an hour repeating all the prayers. I began to feel peaceful when reciting these prayers. Whenever I felt unhappy or disturbed, I would go to a solitary place and recite the Rosary so that I could find a state of happiness and peace. Eventually, I enjoyed reciting the prayers so much that I would often chant them in my mind just to experience a unique feeling of psychic clarity and balance. The recitation of the spiritually-infused words elevated me to a platform where past and future seemed to disappear and the present became vibrant and meaningful due to the closeness I experienced with the Divine.

I was very fortunate to be introduced at such a young age to this process of meditation that allowed me to separate myself from the chatter of the mind.

Sister Patrick believed that prayers constituted a connection to the Lord, and that being attentive to mystic sound strengthened spiritual resolve and reduced mental distractions. She informed me that evil could have power over us if we merely listened to the unrestrained mind. Her simple instructions motivated me to ignore the mind, a discipline which allowed me to experience happiness and clarity of perception.

Learning to Ride the Machine Called "Education"

At the age of five and a half my mother remarried and petitioned the government to have her children released into her and my step-father's custody. The government agreed. A few weeks later we boarded a steamship to England. It was a strange transition from living among nuns to being part of a family with four children. What made the transition even more extreme was leaving

1 / My Personal Story

the sanctuary I had known with the nuns for a far-off land sailing over rough oceans for fourteen days! In England, I attended school for over two years and enjoyed all the activities and interactions of school life. One day the principal called my mother to the school to talk to her about me. After visiting with the principal in his office, my mother came out of the office crying.

The principal had informed her that the British Government had classified me as a "special needs" child. The problem being that during those two school years, I had been unable to learn to read and write. The principal gave my mother a letter and sent her to register me in a special school. My mother and I got into the car and drove to the new school. When we arrived at the school, we noticed that some of the children there appeared to be mentally and physically challenged.

After a short tour of the school, we went back home. My mother told my step-father that the government had determined that I was "retarded" and must therefore attend a special school. She was extremely upset, repeating over and over, "My child is not retarded." Feeling insulted, she called her uncle in South Africa, who arranged passage for our whole family back to Cape Town. After only three years in England, we were now on our way back to South Africa on another fourteen-day steamship journey.

> *"You cannot control the length of your life,
> but you can control its breadth, depth, and height."*
> —Evan Esar

Taking Off the Training Wheels

After arriving back in South Africa, my mother personally tutored me, and in only two months, I was able to read and write. I was placed in a regular government school and scored 95% for my end-of-term math exam and 92% in English. Why did this happen? How did I learn in two months what the British educational system failed to teach me in two years? The answer is that I had become so accustomed to being "in the zone," or in a state of psychic clarity, that I had disconnected from the teachers who were trying to teach me very technical and rote knowledge. Because I had entered so deeply into the realm of the "now" through my connection with spiritual recitation, I had problems balancing the cognitive technical world with the high resolution world of the "now." However, with my mother's determination and gravity, I began to "roll" the influence of the mind back and forth, which allowed the cognitive side of my mind to kick in. My journey to find a way to balance high resolution experiences with the cognitive world had begun. My entire family had to return to South Africa so that I could learn how to use my mind as an instrument! What a wake-up call!

Needless to say, I learned how useful the mind could be, and began to experiment going in and out of psychic clarity at will. I realized that when the mind is properly trained, there is no need to go in and out of the zone. By balanced perception, one can remain in psychic clarity while using the abilities of the mind to focus cognitively. As a young boy, I now began to enjoy the use of this powerful faculty.

My natural state of mind, developed through sacred meditation, allowed me to transcend the effects of enjoyment and distress, where many people seemed at a loss of finding balance, stability, and happiness in the ever-changing field of life. Sister Patrick had been successful in training me earlier in life to find a place of psychic clarity and spiritual peace. I had discovered an internal destination which gave me the steady happiness that the mind alone could not offer.

1 / My Personal Story

Life's Valuable Lessons

I developed an appetite for reading books on ancient teachings as well as mystic poetry. At seventeen I adopted a healthy, alkaline, vegetarian diet and began practicing yoga. I discovered that ancient wisdom had many secrets to happiness and success locked within every word. One of the most profound realizations I had was the need to establish a purpose in my life. I was convinced of the temporary nature of this world, and decided that while I was here I would do something that was meaningful and congruent with my inner beliefs.

I understood that everyone has a different calling in life and that most people had buried their inner-most purpose.

I decided never to sacrifice my purpose in life, but to pursue it with a passion. I wanted to uncover the secrets to inner happiness and knew that if that could be achieved then success would follow like a shadow. Thus began my wonderful journey exploring ancient knowledge and travelling to exotic places where spiritual wisdom was still sewn into the fabric of the culture.

> "There is a kind of 'wild card' within each of us,
> a well of courage and creativity
> we don't even know is in there until we learn how
> to tap into it through spiritual disciplines."
> —Carol Lee Flinders

Empowered Relationships

Whenever I meet spiritual people I am immediately struck by how warm and personal they are. These people always remember your name, and when you speak with them, time seems to stand still. I become riveted in their presence. They are on a different level where everything they say is congruent with their inner beliefs, and you immediately feel comfortable in their association.

It is as if their voice becomes a window into a deeper spiritual reality. I am always taken by how much conviction spiritually-inclined people have in their words. It is impressive how their convictions empower their words and relationships.

I realize that their relationships are empowered because they live in the present and have a perfect balance between their inner beliefs and what they say and do.

I decided to live my life in this way, to become congruent, authentic and passionate about relationships with others.

Sattva Clarity Found

Life happens; nothing can stop time from moving on. It's like learning how to drive a car while it's in motion. No wonder people get confused. Just when we're getting a handle on things, something else pops up.

So it was in my life, while frequently traveling and living in countries with diverse cultures, I learned to become flexible—but there were always surprises. These surprises led me to understand why monks tend to live in protected monasteries with strict routines. This is a way for them to avoid the unpredictable and circumvent the curve balls life throws at you from time to time. They are, in fact, trying to slow down life and stop time. I was always struck by the serenity of temples and ashrams, and how they had succeeded in bringing the "car of life" to a stop while they learned how to master its controls.

1 / My Personal Story

While living in ashrams in India, I learned many of the methods of overcoming inner obstacles from ancient toolboxes. I desired to simplify their tools and codify them so that I could practice them every day under any circumstance. As time went by I began to see how clear my perception of life had become by using these tools. These ancient tools methodically and systematically helped me to think clearly and see things without judgment.

I was struck how things that would normally take me months to achieve were now taking only a few weeks and sometimes only days.

Abundance

Although I practiced a simple lifestyle, the more I realized about life, the richer I felt within. The timeless gems of ancient wisdom made me feel like the most fortunate person. I never once considered myself to be poor. After I married at age twenty-five, I was amazed at how easily I was able to provide with very little effort. Then I realized that the same tools that shaped my life for inner happiness were now shaping my life for outer success. Always optimistic, I enjoyed associating with business people who were also enthusiastic and positive. I discovered that it was their positivity and conviction that the world is full of abundance which drove them to success.

Believing in abundance is the secret that gives life to your goals, relationships, endeavors, and dreams.

Search for Mastery

Even though I was classified as "special needs" by the government school system at the age of seven and a half, I established my first business at age fourteen. By the time I was sixteen, I had studied all the major religions. By seventeen, I began to travel the world, visiting places of pilgrimage in Europe such as Stonehenge and Glastonbury, as well as other Druid and Celtic power centers and Christian cathedrals. I became a monk, living in different spiritual centers throughout Asia, studying Buddhism and Hinduism. After marriage, I started an art business in Singapore, and eventually moved to the United States where I have owned several successful businesses. I still find time to pursue my hobbies, which include travel, photography, aviation and writing.

There is a common misconception that a state of psychic clarity is exclusively for monks and yogis. But with deeper study of ancient texts, I discovered that these practices are meant for everyone.

In fact, previously in the ancient East, this kind of mind control was taught to children from a very early age. It is my hope that soon individuals from all over the world will again be taught how to still the mind to perceive with psychic clarity, so that civilization can advance in leaps and bounds, signaling a dawning of a new age and an upgrade in human consciousness.

There are always difficulties on the path of life, but how we deal with those difficulties makes a significant statement about ourselves. If we search for the light, even in the face of the most dark and depressing circumstances, that light will lead us to the right path. Even in times of crisis, it is important to be able to see things objectively and to make the right decisions.

I discovered that my search for spirituality was also a search for mastery. We find ourselves in this body without an instruction manual. My search was to discover the "Manual for Life," and learn how to master the precious gift of life. Somehow, through decades of searching, I discovered very powerful knowledge that I

1 / My Personal Story

have now distilled into The Seven Powerful Principles.

These tools and principles that brought me success and mastery have also helped many of my friends achieve happiness and success in their lives. This book, and my seminars, provide tangible steps that will guide you to find your purpose in life, enjoy meaningful relationships, become a magnet of success, and achieve mastery in your life. Like the tuning and balancing of the seven *chakra*s in the body, each of the seven chapters dealing with The Seven Powerful Principles will concentrate on and empower the most important aspects of your life.

A Quick Recap

- This chapter described some important milestones in my life, and how I triumphed over adversity by cultivating a mindset of adaptability in *sattva*.
- Challenged in early childhood to adapt to a linear, structured school system, I learned to "grow myself bigger" and have consistently been able to use the lessons learned in order to overcome trying circumstances.
- A large part of my success is due to my ability to learn valuable lessons wherever I find them, whether in the instructions of humble nuns or the writings of ancient saints.
- We all face seemingly insurmountable obstacles in our lives. However, by transforming our consciousness through practicing meditation, rolling back the mind, and using the other tools described in this book, and through my seminars, we can adapt to seemingly insurmountable challenges and emerge happier on the other side.
- Ultimately, obstacles and difficulties are there to strengthen us. Equipped with the proper skills, we can meet them head-on and emerge stronger, not only as individuals, but as a world.

CHAPTER 2

The Secret Power Of Sattva

"What we are looking for is what is looking."
—St. Francis of Assisi

A Lifetime of Searching

TENZEN JAMPA was thirteen years old when he left home to join the local Buddhist monastery. Tenzen had learned respect for the miracles of nature from his mother, and the value of hard work from his father, yet he yearned for more. The year was 1418 and China was ruled by a mighty emperor of the Ming Dynasty. A late beginner (most monks joined the monastery at the age of five or six), Tenzen studied the teachings of Guru Rinpoche. He worked hard at memorizing important *sutras* and *tantras,* and rejoiced when his great teacher awarded him "empowerment" or initiation at the age of sixteen.

Two years later, Tenzen's beloved Guru Rinpoche passed away, and Tenzen felt as if he had been struck by a thunderbolt. Who would be there to encourage him, joke with him, and enlighten him with true knowledge? Amidst his gloom and despair, Tenzen remembered that his guru had instructed him to search out "the bull of happiness." The bull's name, he recalled, was Dharma. Tenzen took this instruction as his life's work. He questioned prominent Lamas (holy persons) on how to find Dharma and then departed for pilgrimage to Lhasa, a holy city in Tibet.

On arriving in Lhasa, Tenzen was struck with wonder. He would listen to enlightening debates in the halls and courtyards of the magnificent monasteries. At night he would light butter lamps, perform sacred rituals, and offer incense in the temple. In the late evening, he would retire to his modest room to study and meditate in the flickering firelight. After two decades of worship and study in Lhasa, Tenzen decided to embark on another journey, vowing to travel until he found Dharma, the mythical bull of happiness, which had continued to elude him. He traveled down wide roads, across roaring rivers, and through narrow mountain passes. Whenever he met someone, he would ask them how to find happiness. Some would tell him that happiness could be found here or there, somewhere or another, or in such-and-such a place. Others told him that only by enjoying the pleasures of this world could happiness be found. Wherever Tenzen went with his begging bowl, he found that people were mostly unhappy. He grew old and weary, unable to locate the mysterious Dharma bull. He prepared to leave his body somewhat regretful of his lack of success in fulfilling the instruction of his spiritual master. As Tenzen lay dying, he noticed his subtle body was mounted on a glowing bull as it slipped out of his physical body—he realized it was Dharma, the bull of happiness, and he had been riding on it his entire life, and now he had eventually found it! Tenzen's life had finally met with success as he fully realized that real happiness was part of his inherent, spiritual nature rather than complex, external, circumstances.

2 / The Secret Power of Sattva

> *"The foolish person seeks happiness in the distance.*
> *The wise grow it under their feet."*
> —James Oppenheim

Have we unconsciously grown to resemble Tenzen, unable to experience constant happiness in our lives because our attention is deviated toward external conditioning? If so, our uncontrolled, out of balance mind will take us on a long, confusing journey perpetually manufacturing new ideas to make us temporarily happy. An out of control mind will steal our essential attentive energy—the key to our happiness.

The purpose of this book is to give you back the key to your happiness and to give you the tools for *sattva* living as well as The Seven Universal Principles for achieving a controlled and blissful state of being.

Sattva Defined

The Sanskrit term *sattva* fully expresses a way of life that promotes a greater depth of living, clearer thinking, and an elevation of consciousness for maintaining perfect balance. The concept of balance is understood more clearly when we learn to accept that we are not a product of our bodies, but rather a transcendent spiritual being experiencing this temporary life through this body.

> *"The wise man is he who has thoroughly understood*
> *that he is spirit soul and not simply a body."*
> —A. C. Bhaktivedanta Swami Prabhupada

Sattva signifies a heightened state of perception, the optimal upgrade of human consciousness. In that elevated state of consciousness, we experience life in higher resolution. We are imbued with indomitable strength, knowledge, magnetism and flexibility.[1]

Becoming sattvic *means to achieve an optimal state of flow through mastering a set of tools that uncover purpose, happiness, and peak performance.*

Inner and outer balance is imperative to success, because although we may be enthusiastic about our purpose in life, when we lack the ability to manage our mental energy, it's likely that we won't achieve our full potential. Through *sattva* we will learn how to switch off mental rants, so that we can attain focus, balance, happiness and success.

Sattva expresses the idea of coming into balance with one's self, and the universe as the key to finding genuine happiness. This is not a new concept, and is deeply rooted within the history of humanity's enlightenment.

An anecdote from the life of Gautama Buddha, the founder of Buddhism, illustrates this idea perfectly. While he was practicing austere meditation and self-deprivation under a tree with other ascetics, the Buddha heard a teacher speaking to his students while on a nearby river boat. The teacher was explaining how to tune a stringed instrument. "If you don't tighten the string enough," the teacher instructed his students, "the sound will be dull, but if you tighten it too much, the string will snap and break. Therefore, you have to tighten it just enough, and then it will emit a sweet melodious sound." Hearing this, Gautama Buddha had a great realization, and at that moment, the Buddha left

---

[1] This explanation of *sattva* is distilled from that found in *Sri Bhagatatatparya-nirnaya* by Madhvacarya (13th century) and *Matsya Purana*.

2 / The Secret Power of Sattva

his ascetic life to practice and teach The Middle Way, a path of moderation between the extremes of unlimited sensual indulgence and harsh self-denial. From The Middle Way, the Buddha developed The Four Noble Truths and The Noble Eightfold Path to Enlightenment. These methods incorporated flexibility, balance, and moderation as processes for achieving perfection and happiness—teachings which essentially embody the principles of *sattva*.

Balance is the Key

Another great personality who devised a system similar to the Buddha's Middle Way was the famous Greek thinker and teacher, Aristotle. Aristotle believed that eudaimonia or happiness can be located as the mean between the deficit and the extreme. Aristotle's ethics grew out of his concept of the mean or middle point. Centuries later, the German philosopher Georg Wilhelm Friedrich Hegel would speak about The Triad of Knowledge, comprised of thesis, antithesis and synthesis. According to a paradigm which Hegel adapted from his philosophical predecessor Immanuel Kant, synthesis is the middle point that is made up of qualities of both thesis and antithesis. The concept of The Middle Way or balance is both popular and powerful. The key point that all these great personalities understood was that from the central pivot of balance, stability flourishes.

What they realized was that by attaining this mental stability we develop a strong sense of security and happiness. It is also from this point of balance that we are least distracted, more efficient, and can access more of our essential, attentive energy.

Tapping Our Psychic Energy

Professor Ronald Heifetz of Harvard suggests that consciousness is capable of "getting bigger." By making an adaptive transformation and by becoming more efficient in the use of certain mental processes we are able to expand our consciousness.

In the field of psychology, the term psychic energy as conceived by Sigmund Freud is frequently used to describe our conscious attention. Freud sometimes described our psychic energy in terms of electricity, because like electricity, our consciousness is distributed between many different thoughts and activities. Like electricity, unless properly controlled, a person's consciousness can make someone a passenger on a roller coaster of uncontrolled or, at best, loosely controlled thoughts and actions; the result of not knowing how to control the mind.

Understanding the energy that drives our consciousness gives us a unique advantage for living a successful and happy life. The more we learn to understand and channel this energy, the quicker we attain happiness and success.

Consciousness is like light that becomes more powerful when concentrated into a laser. When we control our minds, we achieve success. Great sages, yogis, and philosophers spend years focusing and developing techniques to sharpen their perception. By achieving a heightened state of awareness through focus and purpose, consciousness begins to bloom. Achieving *sattva* will help you retain your valuable psychic energy. The by-product of controlling the mind is that you conserve valuable psychic capital, gain mastery of mental concentration, and enter a state of happiness sometimes referred to as Flow, Beingness, In the Zone or *sattva*.

2 / The Secret Power of Sattva

This state makes you efficient and focused so that your effort is optimized to achieve your goals and objectives quickly. When we become centered we are more clearly in touch with our true spiritual nature and, therefore, experience its permanent, blissful state.

The principles of *sattva* will help bring our psychic energy into balance and remove the conflicts and diversions that limit our potential. Like a person balancing on a tight rope, we can only make progress once we achieve balance.

Understanding the Mind

Learning to control consciousness, so that it acts for our benefit, starts with understanding the mind. By nature, our mind either accepts or rejects; deciding quickly and often whimsically whether something is important to us or not. For example, let's say that you decide to go on a diet. But not even a few hours later, your mouth starts watering at the smell of your favorite food. The mind tells you to eat the food even though you may not be hungry! Then after gulping down the food, the same mind tells you what a pig you've become because you have eaten, even though you weren't hungry to begin with! In this way, the mind acts like an enemy, although sometimes it can be our best friend. Actually our intelligence is supposed to keep the mind under control, in balance, and in focus; but often the mind bullies the intelligence into submission. So, how do we take control of the mind?

Being in control of our mind through balance, flexibility and moderation is the greatest secret to success in all that we do.

When the mind is out of balance, it will burn up our psychic energy in its attempts to find balance. If we can maintain balance, we will automatically conserve psychic energy that can be effectively used for powerful activities that are consistent with our purpose and goals in life. By conserving our psychic energy or psychic capital, we can then apply this valuable resource to experience life more deeply, and uninterruptedly cultivate the determination needed to succeed.

Who Are the Happiest People in the World?

Sarah Edelman, who spent years as a research psychologist at the University of Technology in Sydney, Australia writes, "The happiest people in the world are those who have the most flexible attitudes."[2] Happy people are flexible and balanced because they don't allow themselves to be limited and constricted by endless, faulty attitudes which the uncontrolled mind has a tendency to take on. Therefore, achieving happiness will become easier for us too, when we also begin to ignore our mind's endless unproductive babble, and proceed instead from the guiding principle of balanced intelligence through using the principles of *sattva*.

According to recent research, anxiety, stress, and depression are the number one problems in modern society. In fact, anxiety, stress and depression have a huge appetite for our psychic capital! These problems are caused by the mind being thrown out of balance by dwelling on the past or future. The imbalance is compounded when the mind holds onto faulty beliefs that obstruct our happiness.

The first step to gaining control of the ON/OFF switch of the mind is to keep our mental balance by becoming flexible, mindful and stress free.

---

[2] Sarah Edelman. *Change Your Thinking: Overcome Stress, Anxiety, and Depression, and Improve Your Life with CBT*. Da Capo Press, 2007.

2 / The Secret Power of Sattva

In other words, we need to keep our mind under control. Wouldn't life be richer if our feelings and emotions were harnessed to support our internal sense of happiness? Wouldn't being in balance conserve our psychic capital so that we could harness this internal resource to enjoy life at a higher level? With the ability to focus our energy, by controlling the mind, we will succeed in creating a satisfying and purpose-driven life.

Just as a child who strives to walk first has to learn how to attain balance through building new muscles and developing new strengths, so too, by consistently attempting to bring ourselves into balance, we naturally develop emotional and intellectual "muscles" to support the areas where we are out of balance.

Unfortunately, if we do not become mindful and develop our emotional and intellectual muscles, stress, anxiety, depression, and other negative emotions will burn up our psychic energy. However, if we strive to attain balance, this energy will be available to empower us with a greater depth of experience and reward us with a vibrant life in high-resolution. By consistently practicing to manage our energy, we will achieve a blissful state of balance.

External Influences on Our Consciousness

The *Vedas* (India's literary body of ancient wisdom) talk extensively about the universal qualities of *tamas, rajas,* and *sattva,* which can be translated as ignorance, passion, and goodness, respectively. These three forces of nature are said to have their influence on human consciousness. These waves of nature are likened to positive or negative magnetic energy. The key is to establish a balance between them. These invisible currents of energy affect our consciousness, and thereby influence our perceptions and attitudes. These waves are something like the biorhythms of nature. *Sattva* is the state between the negative force of *tamas* and the frenzied force of *rajas*. *Sattva* establishes internal mental equilibrium and also protects us from the external forces of nature. Thus, *sattva* enhances the optimum experience of happiness in life, and allows us to remain balanced, even under trying and forceful external influences. (These three waves are discussed in more detail in Chapter 9.)

Sattva: Life in Perfect Balance

Real happiness is not devoid of variety. An important aspect of happiness can be attained when we bring our lives into balance through variety. *Sattva,* at a heightened level of balance, can be likened to a disk revolving on a pivot point. The momentum of the turning disk symbolizes the variety within life. Balance needs to be attained within the ebb and flow of constant variety. No one can continue to do one thing all the time no matter how enjoyable it may appear to be.

Sometimes people tend to think that perfection will be found through isolation and deep meditation. Isolation and meditation were used by ancient yogis to learn how to take control of the mind and advance their consciousness. Once the mind was controlled, a yogi could see spirituality everywhere and act in the world, but not be of the world. Therefore, learning to control the mind was a useful step toward experiencing life at a higher, spiritual resolution.

When we lose touch with the high resolution of the fabric of life and whittle away our energy on anxiety, stress and depression, what happens to us? We begin to feel trapped, and we no longer enjoy the activities and relationships we used to relish. We hardly

2 / The Secret Power of Sattva

ever smile and get angry easily, we think that things will never get better, and we don't express affection and love to others. Still, we continually try to invent new ways to become happy.

Sattva also implies an inner harmony of feminine and masculine. The feminine side of the brain controls emotion and artistic inclinations, while the masculine side is calculative and determined. Therefore, feminine and masculine must be balanced for an optimal life experience. When a person is out of balance with their feminine side, they will frequently be perceived as hard-hearted and aggressive. Conversely, when someone is out of touch with their masculine side, they can seem to be an emotional mess. Therefore, focusing the mind with emotional balance and mental flexibility will lead to an optimum life experience.

Sattva most importantly addresses balancing our inner aspirations with our external endeavors in a healthy and enduring way. Many people have lost the determination to pursue their real vocation in life. To invoke balance means to start working on our aspirations with our psychic capital. Neglecting these aspirations causes frustration, anger and depression. This book will supply you with the secrets to manifest your deeply cherished aspirations.

Practicing a *sattvic* lifestyle of balance, moderation and flexibility will:

1) Free you from stress and depression.
2) Enrich and deepen your perception and experience of life.
3) Allow you to empower your mental state by freeing up your psychic capital.
4) Bring out the inner happiness from your being through purpose.
5) Allow you to focus your energy in fueling your success.

The Seven Principles of Sattva
1) The Triangle of Health
2) Finding Your Purpose
3) Empowering Your Relationships
4) *Sattva* Clarity: Removing Inner Roadblocks
5) Abundance Mindset
6) Being in the Present
7) *Sattva* Mastery

A Quick Recap

- True happiness is part of our inherent spiritual nature, rather than the product of the complex material circumstances that we are perpetually inventing for ourselves and others.
- Purpose and meaning are essential to living a happy and wholesome life.
- In order to reverse the universal phenomenon of continual dissatisfaction, we need to bring our mind under control and into balance.
- Learn to conserve and channel the touchstone of our psychic energy—the key to our future happiness and success, without resorting to high-risk activities, drugs or endless searching.
- There are Seven Universal Principles for achieving a controlled and blissful state of being through *sattva*, a desirable state of consciousness, described in great detail in the ancient texts of India.
- *Sattva* implies an inner harmony of feminine and masculine natures: balancing our inner aspirations with our external endeavors; heightened perception; focused energy; flexibility; moderation; satisfaction and peace.

CHAPTER 3

Principle 1: The Triangle of Health

"Health is the thing that makes you feel that now is the best time of the year."
—Franklin Pierce Adams

"He who has health has hope, and he who has hope has everything."
—Arabian proverb

"Take care of your body. It's the only place you have to live."
—Jim Rohn

I HAVE FOUND THAT keeping healthy requires a holistic and balanced approach. These are the three important cornerstones of good health:

1) A Healthy Balanced Diet
2) Regular Exercise
3) Thoughtfulness, Meditation and Deep Breathing

Having good health may require a lifestyle change. It cannot be a quick diet or a random spout of exercise. A daily regimen of good food, exercise and meditation will transform your body, mind and entire life.

Your body is your base of operations and, therefore, it is most important to keep it healthy, fit, and stress-free.

This section will give some hints on how to transform your activities to improve your health by taking care of your body and mind. At our seminars and workshops we teach people how to cook healthy food and have a daily routine of exercise and meditation. Many people are very interested in changing their eating habits to a healthy organic diet, but don't have the experience or the confidence to do it. Attending our cooking workshops will equip them with the knowledge and experience they need to prepare mouth-watering, healthy food.

The Diet/Health Disconnect

Daily life has become very fast paced, not just for adults but for children too. Everyone wakes up in the morning and there is a mad scramble to get out the door either to school or to work. Cooking and eating good food has been sacrificed due to time constraints. Nutritious food has been replaced with processed fast foods that are unhealthy and give little satisfaction. Our media is flooded with well-sculpted beautiful men and women having six-packs and flawless bodies and celebrities showing off their slim waists and breast implants. These professionals make a living keeping their bodies in perfect shape on the outside, either by good diet and exercise or going under the knife and hiding their bulimia, while ordinary people are struggling to keep up.

3 / Principle 1: The Triangle of Health

The problem is that if we consume the products that dominate television, magazines and our local supermarket, we will not end up looking like those celebrities, but rather like victims of commercialization.

When we say we live in a consumer society, it means that big corporations and government grow rich from what we consume. The problem is, we are being cheated. Everything that we consume, the necessities of life, will be delivered to us at the cheapest cost to them, and the highest price to us. Whether it is your electricity or your food, the corporations will sacrifice your health, and the health of the planet, so that they can make a profit.

> "Health is not just the absence of disease.
> It's an inner joyfulness that should be ours all the time,
> a state of positive well-being."
> —Deepak Chopra

Stuck Between the Media and the Healthcare System

The media pushes us to consume food products that corporations have vigilantly processed to be lifeless, then when we get sick, the doctors treat the symptoms and not the cause. Therefore, it is important to have a clear understanding of what foods are good for our bodies. We should not be fooled by great packaging and media hype, or satisfied with treating the symptoms and not the cause. Rather we should be determined to educate ourselves to what foods are good for our children and ourselves.

Currently, the leading causes of death are heart disease, cancer, cerebrovascular disease (caused by hypertension and stress), diabetes, Alzheimer's disease and influenza. All of these, except influenza, take years to develop. What is the common denominator between these diseases, and how can we avoid them? Scientific research is proving that these diseases are diet and stress-related.

In this chapter, you will learn how diet and lifestyle changes can help protect your body and mind from deadly diseases. You will learn simple adjustments to your diet that will protect you from chronic imbalances.

The High Cost of Our Low-Cost Foods

Understanding and controlling diet is a powerful step that you can take in transforming your entire life. Therefore, it is important to constantly endeavor to maintain and improve your diet.

When we see food in the supermarkets with designer packaging and brand names, it is easy to forget that most food processing companies do not care about our health. In fact many of these companies are putting products in our food that will become detrimental to our health over time.

One Example: High Fructose Corn Syrup (HFCS)

For example, high fructose corn syrup (HFCS) is an artificial sweetener that was created in laboratories in Japan. This sweetener costs much less than sugar to produce and is much sweeter. Because of its cheap cost, manufacturers have been putting it into food for decades. Unfortunately, it is metabolized by the liver in the same way as ethanol or alcohol, and is therefore a toxin. The worst side-effect of HFCS is that it confuses the hormone, Leptin. Leptin is the hormone that regulates metabolism; it tells us when we are hungry or full. For example, if you drink a soda (with HFCS in it) while you're eating, even though you may have consumed over a 1,000 calories, the HFCS confuses your brain so that it still feels dissatisfied.

Not only does HFCS trick your body so that it still feels hungry

3 / Principle 1: The Triangle of Health

even when you've eaten enough, it is also highly toxic to your liver. After ingesting HFCS, it is metabolized in your liver, to produce VHDL (very-high density-lipoprotein) which causes high blood pressure and contributes to heart disease. Please watch the informative YouTube[3] video of Dr. Robert H. Lustig, MD, UCSF Professor of Pediatrics in the Division of Endocrinology & Metabolism. Dr. Lustig gives convincing arguments in his presentation called, "The Bitter Truth."

Bisphenol-A: The Resin in the Lining of Tin Cans

Bisphenol-A (BPA) is a resin used to coat the inside of tin cans. The European Union and Canada have banned BPA, as it is considered a toxic substance since it exerts detectable hormone properties. Japan also recently banned the use of BPA in canned foods. This resin, that is also used in many plastic bottles and coats the inside of tin cans in the United States, has the most devastating effects on early developing children and fetuses since it is an endocrine disruptor. In 2006, the US Government sponsored an assessment of the scientific literature on BPA. Thirty-eight experts on endocrine disrupters gathered in Chapel Hill, North Carolina to review several hundred studies on BPA. At the end of the meeting, the panel of experts came up with the Chapel Hill Consensus Statement, which stated "BPA at concentrations found in the human body is associated with organizational changes in the prostate, breast, testis, mammary glands, body size, brain structure and chemistry, and behavior of laboratory animals."[4] Dr. Frederick vomSaal, PhD., an Endocrinologist at the University of Missouri, believes that the acidity found in canned toma-

---

[3] http://www.youtube.com/watch?v=dBnniua6-oM
[4] http://en.wikipedia.org/wiki/Bisphenol_A

toes causes BPA to leach into the food faster. Studies show that the BPA in most people's bodies exceeds the amount that suppresses sperm production or causes chromosomal damage to the eggs of animals. "You can get 50 mcg of BPA per liter out of a tomato can, and that's a level that is going to impact people, particularly the young," says vomSaal. "I won't go near canned tomatoes."[5] The alternative is to buy glass-bottled tomatoes or Tetra Pak containers.

Another Example: High Cholesterol

The next time you feel like eating fast food, think again. The body is a complex mechanism that is always trying to keep in balance. One of the biggest concerns these days is the level of cholesterol in our blood. Cholesterol has a large number of uses in the body and we depend on its production for optimum health, however, there are two types of cholesterol: the good type High-Density Lipoprotein (HDL) and the bad type Low-Density Lipoprotein (LDL).

The liver produces our daily cholesterol requirements, and the blood transports the cholesterol fats around the body for use in cells and other organisms. The problem is that if the LDL (bad cholesterol) becomes disproportionate to the HDL (good cholesterol), the surplus of LDL begins to wreak havoc in our bodies. Excess cholesterol gets deposited on artery walls. This build-up causes blockages that can lead to angina or a heart attack. When built-up cholesterol, in the form of plaque, flakes off from the blocked arterial walls, these flakes of plaque can cause strokes, or occlusion of the coronary artery leading to a heart attack. Choles-

---

[5] http://www.prevention.com/food/healthy-eating-tips/7-foods-should-never-cross-your-lips/1-canned-tomatoes#ixzz1rr0QoXQn

terol build-up also contributes to many common diseases.

If you are following an eating pattern that is high in processed sugars, you will produce more insulin and, therefore, may have a problem with excess cholesterol. Insulin also stimulates synthesis of triglycerides which get stored in your body as fat. Artificial sweeteners and too many carbohydrates without fiber intake will become stored in the body as fat.

By following a mostly alkaline diet with fresh vegetables, fruits, whole grains, carbohydrates, and a balanced amount of protein, you allow the liver to de-stress and take a major step in the direction of having the proper cholesterol ratio and amount in your body.

A Healthy Diet: The Real Solution

Buy organic products as much as possible. If you eliminate all sweetened drinks and drink pure water or milk many of your health problems will be solved. Take the time to understand why excess proteins and processed carbohydrates have a negative impact on your health, and reduce them from your diet.

Cook your own food if possible. Steaming vegetables rather than frying them will improve your digestion. Eating small meals more frequently aids your metabolism and puts less stress on your digestive system. Try to completely avoid soda drinks and any type of sweetened drinks that have no fiber. Smoothies using real fruit will be healthier for your body than any drinks purchased in the store. Companies that make beverages remove important fiber because it shortens shelf-life.

The two most frequently sprayed foods:
Potatoes are frequently treated with fungicides and herbicides that get absorbed into the vegetable. Later when they are dug up

they are yet again treated to prevent them from sprouting. Nonorganic apples are individually grafted from a single tree; they don't develop resistance to pests, and are the most frequently doused-in-pesticide fruit there is.

Farm workers have higher rates for many cancers, and recent studies are starting to link Parkinson's disease with a higher body-burden of pesticides.

татр: It is good policy to buy all your fresh produce organic. But at the least buy only organic potatoes and apples.

TIP: It is good policy to buy all your fresh produce organic. But at the least buy only organic potatoes and apples.

While eating, try not to watch TV, or drive, or do anything else that taxes your mind or body. If you focus on the taste of the food while you are eating, you will be much more satisfied at the end of your meal. If you are distracted while eating, you will feel less satisfied, and will want to nibble on more and more food, since the mind is not yet satisfied.

Since stress stimulates insulin production, which results in excess cholesterol in the blood, avoid stress at all costs. Studies have shown that stress and bad diet have devastating effects on your health.

Healthy eating is a lifestyle change not a temporary diet.

Quick Nutrition 101

Vitamins and Minerals

Vitamins and minerals are essential for good health and facilitate necessary chemical reactions in the body. The best source of these nutrients is from fresh organic fruits and vegetables. Most vitamins sold over the counter are artificially produced in labs and don't come from fresh produce. If you eat a healthy diet, then there may be no need of supplementary vitamins. If you do take them, stick to the proper daily dosage and use a brand that makes their supplements from real food sources. Remember that this billion dollar industry is, for the most part, just another way to take your money while fooling you into believing that you are massively improving your health.

Most of the vitamins you may consume will pass through you within a day because your body only needs minute quantities. The necessary amount of vitamins and minerals are readily available in a daily diet of fresh produce. Minerals have many different functions in the body and are also needed in small doses. Minerals are metals that come from the earth, and are delivered to us through our food. Calcium, potassium, sodium, phosphorus, magnesium, etc., are vital for the proper health of the body and are available when we eat fresh vegetables, fruits, grains, and dairy.

Proteins

Proteins are essential building blocks for our bodies and are especially important while children are growing. With the protein craze in food products and high protein diets, people are overloading their bodies with protein. Protein is a great source of energy, but when we consume it in excess, the body will use what it needs and convert the rest to be stored as fat and sugar. When protein derived from meat is broken down by our metabolism, uric acid is released which is extremely toxic for the body.

Certain amino acids in protein leach calcium from bones, therefore, societies that consume large quantities of meat and milk products have a higher incidence of arthritis and osteoporosis. The key point is that unless you are a professional athlete or a growing child, you should have moderate amounts of protein in your diet. Even vegans, who eat no animal protein will get twice as much protein as their body needs. If you do overload your body with protein, remember it will increase the size of your waistline and arms.

Fiber

In order for food corporations to sell their goods, they have to achieve the longest shelf-life possible for their products. Fiber reduces shelf-life; therefore, food companies remove this vital ingredient from their foods. To maintain a healthy body we require 25 to 30 grams of fiber daily. If you are eating mostly processed food your body will lack fiber. Juice from the supermarket has the fiber removed, so even though you think it is healthy, actually it is mostly flavored fructose water.

When you consume fructose without fiber it digests differently in your body and burdens your liver. Lack of fiber causes constipation and results in unhealthy bowels. Eating fresh vegetables and fruit will give you all the fiber you need and will keep your body healthy. It is better to drink water or milk if you are thirsty. If you like fruit juice, blend fresh fruits and drink them with the pulp.

Enzymes

The body uses enzymes for every function and activity. They are the building blocks of life and maintain the vitality of the body by their presence. Without them we could not survive. We use enzymes for digestion, maintenance, repair and every chemical action in our body. Fruits and vegetables have natural enzymes. Eating fresh fruits and vegetables high in enzymes aids our digestion.

When foods are cooked or processed at a temperature over 116°, all the enzymes are destroyed. Food manufacturers destroy the enzymes in the processing. The absence of enzymes extends the shelf-life of the food, but puts more of a burden on our digestion. When foods have no digestive enzymes, the body has to supply enzymes to digest the food. Since the pancreas supplies a lot of these enzymes, having a consistent diet of processed foods can lead to diabetes. Therefore, it is vitally important to be aware of the dangers of maintaining a diet high in processed foods. Try to eat fresh vegetables that are lightly steamed. This will maintain the natural enzymes that are extremely useful for maintaining a strong digestion and healthy body.

> *"To be a vegetarian is to disagree—*
> *to disagree with the course of things today.*
> *Nuclear power, starvation, cruelty—*
> *we must make a statement against these things.*
> *Vegetarianism is my statement.*
> *And I think it's a strong one."*
>
> —Isaac Bashevis Singer

An Inconvenient Truth: Diet and the Environment

Keep in mind that eating natural, organic, unprocessed food will not only be good for your body, but ultimately will be good for the earth. It is our moral obligation to become stewards of our environment so that future generations can enjoy a vibrant, healthy planet.

If we are to be stewards of the environment, it makes perfect sense to follow an alkaline vegetarian diet, since a meat based diet cannot be sustained by the environment and the planet.

A report called "Livestock in a Changing Landscape"[6] from an international research team exploring the global impact of the livestock industry on the environment has these stunning figures. Livestock for human consumption uses 26% of the earth's terrestrial surface. A further 33% of global arable land is used to grow feed for global livestock. Natural forests are being replaced to accommodate grazing for raising cattle for humans to feed on. For example 70% of former forests in the Amazon have been destroyed and turned over for grazing. The livestock sector accounts for 9% of all carbon dioxide emissions derived from human-related activities, as well as 37% of methane emissions—primarily gas from the digestive system of cattle and other domesticated ruminants—and 65% of nitrous oxide gases, mostly from manure.

According to the report, the global livestock sector produces 65% of human related nitrous-oxide, which has approximately 300 times the Global Warming Potential (GWP) than CO_2. It produces 37% of human induced methane (23 times GWP than CO_2).

The livestock industry degrades land and water resources faster than anything else on the planet.

Harold A. Mooney, Professor of Biology at Stanford University, and Senior Fellow at the Woods Institute for the Environment,

---

[6] "Livestock in a Changing Landscape" is a collaboration of the FAO, SHL, Woods Institute for the Environment, International Livestock Research Institute (ILRI), Scientific Committee for Problems of the Environment (SCOPE), Agricultural Research Center for International Development (CIRAD), and Livestock, Environment and Development Initiative (LEAD).

and co-editor of the report said, "The livestock industry is massive and growing." This is a disturbing statement considering the impact this industry has on the environment.

In order to produce one pound of meat, it takes sixteen pounds of grain to be grown as feed. With an average weight of 1,100 pounds at slaughter, this translates to 17,600 pounds of grain to bring one mature beef cow to market. In a world where 1.3 billion people directly or indirectly derive their livelihood from the meat industry, imagine how much food could be grown for human consumption if these resources were harnessed for grains, vegetables and fruits for human consumption. I am sure starvation would become a thing of the past.

Most governments on the planet subsidize the meat industry. For example, in America, if meat was not subsidized the lowest grade hamburger meat would cost $32 a pound.

With these staggering statistics and a concern for the environment, it makes perfect sense to adopt vegetarian based diets. Using 33% of arable land to feed cattle, when sixteen pounds of grain only produces one pound of meat, is a complete waste of arable land.

If our civilization continues on the path of wholesale exploitation of our environment and neglect for Mother Nature, there will be far reaching repercussions not just for our personal health, but for the health of the whole planet. When we experience the benefit of a healthy organic lifestyle, it is our obligation to share that experience with our fellow human beings.

My personal path to vegetarianism happened after reading descriptions in the *Vedas* of ancient civilizations that lived harmonious and organic lifestyles; where livestock, namely the cow and bull, were used to plow the fields and produce milk and milk products. We can receive plenty of protein through milk, cheese, yogurt and other milk products that are rich in animal fat. Milk is produced out of love. The cow transforms her blood into milk out of love for her calf. By nature's plan, she produces more milk than the calf needs, and therefore, there is enough left over for human consumption. I could not come to terms with the idea of these gentle animals giving up their lives so that I could consume their flesh. Surprisingly, I found a vegetarian diet made me more energetic, less lethargic and gave me clarity of thought.

Physical Fitness and Exercise

> *"If it weren't for the fact that the TV set and the refrigerator are so far apart, some of us wouldn't get any exercise at all."*
>
> —Joey Adams

Becoming fit facilitates your body's need to perform regular activities and maintains optimum health. Becoming fit does not mean becoming a professional athlete, neither does it mean taking a walk once a week. Rather, fitness is a daily process of maintaining flexibility and muscle tone in your body. If you maintain this daily routine, you should not have excess fat on your body, and should enjoy full mobility throughout your life.

One of the tips to maintaining a regular exercise regimen is to find an activity that you enjoy doing daily and that gives you a full workout.

It may be taking regular yoga or martial arts classes, swimming or getting involved in community sports. There are unlimited activities that can become a regular workout for you. So go out, join a gym or yoga school, and subscribe to health and fitness magazines. Any regular form of physical exercise you do will make a vast improvement to the quality of your life and your health.

3 / Principle 1: The Triangle of Health

If you prefer to spend most of your time at home, there are software programs and DVDs with guided exercises to follow. These software programs have tailored exercise regimens for your body type and track your progress on a daily basis. Taking a walk daily can be great exercise and a wonderful meditation. My financial advisor, Lewis, walks daily for just under an hour and finds that this daily exercise routine has become an oasis of spiritual realization for him. He explained to me one day how his daily walks have helped him become more balanced and connected to nature, the walks have become a meditation as well as a daily routine of exercise.

I enjoy yoga because it constantly challenges me to improve. Although the positions may be hard to master at first, over time they become easier. Yoga also helps concentrate consciousness and puts you in touch with your purpose. Combined with the breathing exercises in the Power Meditation (which I describe in this chapter), I find myself feeling fully vitalized both physically and mentally every day. Yoga and Power Meditation are two of the most popular classes at our seminars.

It is important to understand how your body works, so read books on fitness, and understand how your muscles and tendons work. If you are a member of a gym try to get some private coaching time. Associate with people who are engaged regularly in exercising. Join a cycling group with people in your neighborhood or form a group that jogs on a daily basis. Your choice of exercise is a personal preference that could range from tennis, cycling and mountaineering to weight lifting, martial arts, walking and yoga. There are many activities that will keep your limbs moving and the blood circulating. Remember that if you don't use the capabilities of your body, you may lose them.

> "*An early morning walk is a blessing for the whole day.*"
> —Henry David Thoreau

> "*Those who think they have not time for bodily exercise will sooner or later have to find time for illness.*"
> —Edward Stanley

Peter Burwash, a professional athlete and fitness guru, has given physiological reasons why exercise is important to the health of your body. Below is an excerpt from his excellent book Total Health: The Next Level[7] giving twenty eye-opening reasons to keep your limbs moving. I would recommend getting a copy of his book as it covers all aspects of diet and exercise.

Top Twenty Advantages of Exercise

1. *Flushes Poisons Out of the Body*. During exercise, your body temperature rises several degrees. This helps kill bacteria. When you exercise, your body releases the same proteins it does when it is fighting bacteria, and it produces a higher number of white cells. Toxins are also released through perspiration. And, finally, during an aerobic workout, poisons are released through the mouth.

2. *Stimulates Immune System*. Exercise helps muscles contract to push fluid through the one-way valves. Sitting down or inactivity slows circulation and stagnates the blood.

3. *Reduces Amount of Fat in the Body*. Apart from the fact that excess fat is damaging to your health, fat stores many toxins. Exercise literally "turns on" your metabolism and liberates calories.

---

[7] Peter Burwash, *Total Health: The Next Level* (Life Enrichment Library, Torchlight Publishing, 1997), p. 76–79. Inserted with permission from publisher.

4. *Strengthens Lungs and Heart.* Life is movement, and the heart craves exercise. When the heart is strong, it beats less often. Since there is no way to exercise the heart, lungs, and blood vessels directly, exercise places a demand on the cardiovascular system. Lack of exercise makes one two times more likely to develop coronary heart disease (Center for Disease Control).

5. *Raises Basic Metabolic Rate.* This means you will burn more calories—not only during a workout, but also while at rest. The metabolic rate can remain elevated for up to twelve hours after exercise.

6. *Increases Number of Red Blood Cells.* More red blood cells increase the carrying capacity of oxygen to the muscles. Therefore, you don't quit as soon.

7. *More Oxygen to the Cells.* The purpose of exercise is to get oxygen to cells. If cells don't get oxygen, they die. The muscles of a physically fit person are better able to extract oxygen from circulating blood.

8. *Stronger Bones.* Bones strengthen and thicken, just like muscles, when exercised or subjected to heavy loads or gravity. Tennis players always have bigger bones in the arm they play with. This is important to know, as there are still too many people who think they get stronger bones by pouring vast amounts of calcium into their body.

9. *Builds Up Muscles.* There are approximately 630 muscles in the body, and if you don't use them, they atrophy. The human body actually breaks down when it is not being used. So, the more you use your muscles, the better they get. A well-exercised bicep doesn't deteriorate; it gets stronger.

10. *Peripheral Circulation Increased.* This is a big one, because alternate routes for blood are opened up in the event the main artery is blocked. This may save your life.

11. *Keeps Joints More Mobile.* There is less degeneration of joints. Too many people rust out too soon.

12. *Raises HDL (The Good Cholesterol).* HDL is believed to be an arterial cleanser.

13. *Reduces Potential Cancer Risks.* Scientists believe that exercise reduces the risk of cancer by causing good activity in the colon, whereby food moves out of the body at a faster rate. In talking with doctors in the East, they all believed this to be one of the principal keys to good health.

14. *Appetite Depressed After Exercise.* This usually occurs for one to two hours following the exercise. It limits the craving and desire to eat more.

15. *Helps Store More Glycogen.* A fit person stores more glycogen in the muscle (between ten to fifty percent more than an unfit person) and, thus, gains a greater ability for endurance workouts.

16. *Helps Overcome Weariness.* The best remedy for fatigue or weariness is usually a thirty-minute aerobic workout.

17. *Higher Tolerance for Fatigue.* When you're fit, you "hang tougher" under crises.

18. *Promotes Clearer and More Rational Thought.* When in shape, you focus on things rationally rather than emotionally. Physical inactivity seems to make the mind go dull. Exercise helps to "clean the static from the attic."

19. *Less Clotting of the Blood.* Exercise makes the blood platelets less sticky and less likely to clog.

20. *Releases Nature's Tranquilizers* (endorphins). Also called mood elevators, endorphins are responsible for a sense of well-being and the euphoric feeling we experience after a good workout.

The Effects of Stress—Baboons and Civil Servants

Two very important studies showing parallel results have become the "Rosetta Stone" for deciphering the link between stress and disease. These studies are "The Robert Sapolsky Thirty-Year Field Study of Wild African Baboons" and "The Whitehall I and II Studies of Civil Servants in the UK."

Robert Sapolsky's studies are very interesting because baboons live similar lives to humans. They only have to forage for food for about three hours a day, they don't have many problems with predators, they live in interdependent groups, and a good deal of their time is spent generating psychological stress toward other baboons in their troop!

Sapolsky's study found that there was a direct link between the hierarchy in the troop of baboons and the amount of stress hormones in their blood. The dominant males in the group had less stress hormones in their blood, whereas the low-ranking baboons were more susceptible to stress and had higher levels of stress hormones in their blood. The low-ranking baboons were frequently harassed and put under a lot of stress by the high-ranking, dominant males. The low-ranking baboons developed stress-related diseases, their reproduction system didn't work well, wounds healed slowly and they had high blood pressure. Many of them lived shorter lives and suffered from obesity and coronary atherosclerosis. The dominant baboons, however, lived longer, did not get sick as often, were more physically fit and had stronger immune systems. Keep in mind that both the dominant baboons and the low-ranking baboons shared the same diet and exercise regimen.

The two Whitehall studies were conducted between 1967 and 2007 among 10,000 civil servants in England. Working in the Civil Service is considered a steady career. All civil servants enjoy the same medical benefits and most of them keep their jobs throughout their lives. These remarkable studies revealed an astonishing similarity to Sapolsky's studies. Lower-ranking civil servants were associated with higher risk factors, which included obesity, more baseline illness, higher blood pressure, a 2 to 1 ratio of cardiovascular disease mortality, and greater incidence of depression.

These two studies give clear proof that stress is one of the highest contributing factors to disease. Being in a stressful workplace, where you are not in control of your environment or workload and are under a lot of pressure from higher-ranking workers, can increase sickness and reduce your lifespan.

Stress hormones such as cortisol and norepinephrine affect the metabolic system and also play a role in depression, hypertension and Attention Deficit Hyperactivity Disorder (ADHD). An imbalance in these hormones, due to stress, can play havoc on the body.

Mothers Aging Six Times Faster

Elizabeth Blackburn, Nobel Prize Laureate and Professor of Biology and Physiology at UCSF (University of California at San Francisco), led a team of researchers who studied fifty-eight mothers in a study called "Accelerated Telomere Shortening in Response to Life Stress." Half of the mothers were caring for children with chronic disorders such as autism and cerebral palsy. Researchers studied the telomere connectors of DNA from the white blood cells in these mothers' blood. What they found was quite telling. The telomeres of the mothers who were caring for children with disabilities had aged and frayed six times more than those of mothers with normal children. This showed that they were aging from a DNA level six times faster due to the stress of caring for a special needs child. As this erosion was taking place in their white blood cells, it was compromising their immune systems. Elizabeth Blackburn also discovered the enzyme telomerase, which makes telomere DNA. Telomerase is produced to mend or maintain the telomere connectors in the DNA's replication process in human immune system cells.

Elizabeth Blackburn's studies showed how people who are under stress have weaker immune systems and are actually aging quicker.

Solutions to Stress

Dr. Dean Ornish, a pioneer in lifestyle intervention to reduce cardiovascular disease, recently did studies of thirty men with low-risk prostate cancer. He prescribed a low-fat, low-refined sugar diet with ample unrefined grains, fruits and vegetables. Vitamin supplements were provided; moderate aerobic exercise, stress management, relaxation techniques and breathing exercises were encouraged. It was found that twenty-four of the thirty men studied had a 30% increase in telomerase enzyme activity. Ornish's research means that through lifestyle changes, the immune system can be boosted, and DNA aging can be reduced, and even reversed.

From the studies above, we learn that if we want to remain healthy, we have to learn how to identify stress and avoid it. Changing your lifestyle into a more balanced and stress-free one is the best way to avoid stress-related disease.

One of the most effective techniques for reducing stress is to learn how to relax and practice bringing your body and mind into peace and balance through meditation. The more a person undergoes stress, pain and suffering, the more rapidly they begin to breath. By learning how to slow down and regulate our breath, we begin to establish balance and discharge harmful stress and anxiety.

Meditation and Breathing

> *"Meditation is not an evasion;
> it is a serene encounter with reality."*
> —Thich Nhat Hanh

> *"Like water which can clearly mirror the sky
> and the trees only so long as its surface is undisturbed,
> the mind can only reflect the true image of the self
> when it is tranquil and wholly relaxed."*
> —Indra Devi

> *"Within you there is a stillness and sanctuary
> to which you can retreat at any time and be yourself."*
> —Hermann Hesse (*Siddharta*)

Meditation is the practice of stilling the mind and experiencing the peace and joy within. Interestingly, I have found that by dedicating some quiet time on a daily basis for meditation, I actually have more time for other things. I will introduce you to a meditation I developed called Power Meditation. This meditation will empower your life by connecting you to *sattva* through your breath.

Power Meditation is a combination of meditation with deep breathing exercises. Power Meditation will do wonders for calming your mind and keeping your body healthy. Oxygenating your blood and body through deep breathing can help balance your body's hormones and increase Alpha and Beta brain waves. *Pranayama* or breathing meditation is said to reduce cortisol, the stress hormone, as well as to increase anti-oxidants and strengthen the immune levels in the body. It increases your vitality and rewards you with an immediate feeling of the energy of *sattva*.

Power Meditation Step-by-Step:

1. Choose a time when you are free from disturbances.
2. Find a comfortable place to sit.
   - Use a yoga mat for sitting cross-legged or a chair with good lumbar support.
   - Watch the sunrise or gaze out over the ocean, or you may prefer to sit inside or under a tree.
   - Wherever you decide to sit, make sure you feel comfortable.
3. Relax your body.
   - Start by loosening your shoulders and neck.
   - Make sure your hands and legs are in a comfortable position. (I find that doing a sequence of yoga postures helps to increase flexibility and relax my whole body.)
4. Relax the mind with deep breathing.
   - Start with slow, heavy breathing and listen to the sound of the in and out breaths.
   - Visualize the incoming breath empowering your *sattva* state, and the outgoing breath expelling the agitation of the mind.
   - Make sure you are doing deep breathing from the chest. You should feel your chest moving.
   - Begin to speed your breath up so that its pace be comes twice that at which you normally breathe.
   - Center your consciousness on the breath.
   - If your mind begins to wander, relax it and bring it in- to focus on the sound, and feeling of the deep breathing.

- Be absorbed in the inward and outward breath.
- While the inward breath brings you closer and deeper toward yourself, the outward breath discharges stress and distances the mind.
- Breathe in and out deeply like this for approximately three minutes, or until your chest feels tired.

5. Now take in a deep breath and hold it.
   - Hold it for as long as you can.
   - Experience the peace and tranquility of your inner self.
   - You will feel a deep connection with self and experience the vibrancy of life.
6. When you feel the need to breathe again
   - Begin another cycle of approximately three minutes of breathing.
7. Continue these cycles for the length of your allotted time.
8. As you become calmer, don't allow the mind to begin a dialogue about your experience.
   - The mind will try to give its commentary, but push all those thoughts out with the exhalation of breath.
   - Sometimes you may feel like you are entering into a dreaming state, but again bring the focus back to the breathing.
   - Use all your psychic bandwidth to experience the breathing and the effect it has on you.

You will begin to experience *sattva* as your consciousness resonates free from the mind. Try to maintain this feeling of connective vibration with the universe. Within days, you will begin to feel a more permanent, general sense of joy from within, lasting throughout your day. It will come out of you slowly as the process of Power Meditation begins to heal inner wounds and blockages. All the self-judgments, conditions, barriers and false identifications will fade away. You will begin to feel your true, powerful self.

Begin by doing Power Meditation for fifteen minutes a day and only increase when the quality has increased. It is better to do fifteen minutes of good Power Meditation, which enables you to enter into pure *sattva,* than to spend two hours doing poor Power Mediation listening to an uncontrolled mind. Eventually you will be able to increase your meditation time in a way that is practical for you.

Meditating at different times of the day can enhance your experience. Sunrise is a great time to do Power Meditation. The experience of a new day surging with energy as the sun majestically rises over the horizon is extremely energizing, while Power Meditation late at night during the full moon will pacify and relax the mind. Your *sattva* state will emerge like the rising full moon empowering your consciousness. Sunset is also a wonderful time. As the coming of night signals a time of rest, so should we also seek peace and still the chattering and ranting of the mind. As darkness covers the world, we look within to the light of *sattva,* and bask in its warmth and bliss.

With a regular and steady commitment to improving and strengthening your sattva *state, you will find peace and contentment.*

During the day, even though you may be very busy, you will be able to bring your mind under control by listening to the sound of your breathing. You will be fully satisfied simply with presence. You will not depend on external conditions for happiness. You will develop a taste for the positive feelings of *sattva* and presence.

Soon you will realize that there is little value to the mental commentary of your mind. The only value is in true perception of you, the world, and others.

When true perception arises, balance will become an automatic by-product, just as the rising sun is always followed by illumination in all directions. No separate endeavor is needed: charity will be balanced with success, fame balanced with serving through philanthropy, strength balanced with protection, and knowledge balanced with humility.

All of the psychic energy that was being used to maintain mental equilibrium will now be reserved. If you allow your mind to take control again, you will immediately feel the sapping of your psychic energy. Becoming conscious of your psychic energy level is important because you will begin to value its potency. Psychic energy is powerful; it is condensed creative energy. It empowers your efforts and magnifies your perception exponentially.

> *"What we cultivate in times of ease,
> we gather as strength in times of change."*
> —the Buddha

Music As a Tool for Transformation and De-Stressing

Certain types of music have a magical effect on our mood, both triggering and enhancing positive feelings. Music can help us relax and dissipate stress and fatigue. Music is a powerful tool which can alter emotions, and therefore, the brain itself.

> *"Without music, life is a journey through a desert."*
> —Pat Conroy

3 / Principle 1: The Triangle of Health

In-depth research on the neurological effects of music still needs to be undertaken. Since music and its effects are very subjective, it might seem difficult to unite these mutually exclusive fields of biology and melody. However, according to an article in *The Economist* (February 12–18, 2000) entitled "The Biology of Music":

> Music's effect on the outer layers of the brain—the temporal and even the visual cortex—is only half the story . . . These are the places in which the signal is being dissected and processed. The place where it is having its most profound effect is in the brain's emotional core—the limbic system.

Emotional response to music has been shown to affect hormone levels in the body. Some research shows evidence that music lowers levels of cortisol in the body. Cortisol is present in the body whenever we experience stress. The reason music relaxes us is largely due to increased levels of melatonin in the body. Melatonin induces relaxation, and helps to re-adjust the body's internal clock and remedy the effects of jetlag, for instance.

Just as Hollywood producers are very particular about the soundtracks they compose for their movies, so too should we be selective about the music we listen to, and its effects on us.

> "Music washes away from the soul the dust of everyday life."
> —Berthold Auerbach

Many people feel they can't live without their music. Music has the ability to brighten our day and inspire us when we wake up in the morning. Music has the ability to revive memories of the past. It is such a powerful medium that we can almost smell, see and feel experiences that may have happened long ago, when we hear music that evokes our past.

Waking up early can be difficult, but being slowly awakened by sweet music certainly helps. When I was a young boy, my father used to play a recording of a beautiful symphony early in the morning to rouse us from sleep. Ingeniously, my dad constructed an elaborate arrangement by rigging an alarm clock to a vinyl record player. Somehow at the right time, the clock would trigger the record player to drop the record on the turntable and start playing a composition by Bach or Tchaikovsky. Thankfully, due to the digital revolution, it is not difficult to set up such an arrangement nowadays. As MP3 players are frequently embedded into cell phones and alarm clocks, it is just a matter of clicking a few buttons and voila! Programming an alarm to play your favorite inspiring track when it awakens you from sleep can set the tone for the rest of your day.

When doing your daily yoga or exercise, you may choose to play some relaxing music, or play something "high energy" if you are working out in a gym. It is up to you to decide what music motivates you to maintain and improve upon a daily routine. Music works wonders if you're relaxing in a bath or hot tub. Music can help you unwind, and also sensitize you to appreciate silence.

A much better alternative to the dangerous practice of texting while driving is to listen to your favorite music while driving. Rush hour traffic affects many drivers who get agitated and frustrated by having to continually stop and start. Selective music, with its calming rhythms, induces a consistent feeling of happiness that overrides the negative effects of the traffic. And playing music will usually make guests or friends feel comfortable immediately. When entertaining guests, it is always a good idea to find out in advance what their favorite piece of music is, and then to make an effort to play it. Playing their favorite music can make your friends and associates feel comfortable.

The ancient sages of India knew that music has the power to magnify human emotion. In fact, they believed that particular ragas (melodies) were the personification of a specific feeling or emotion. We too can use music as a tool in our program of success. At our seminars, attendees experience first-hand the power of music. We also have powerful guided meditations on CD using music as a tool to empower and unlock positive emotions. These guided meditations help overcome fears and phobias, build confidence, strengthen relationships, unlock inherent happiness and have a very positive and dynamic effect on the listeners.

With music, it is possible to enhance your emotional state, to relax and relieve stress. The more you become aware of the effects of music, the more you will be able to harness them in your own life and the lives of others.

> "Music is a higher revelation than philosophy."
> —Ludwig van Beethoven

> "After silence, that which comes nearest
> to expressing the inexpressible is music."
> —Aldous Huxley

A Quick Recap

- Your health is affected primarily by three factors: the food you eat, how much you exercise, and the amount of stress to which you allow yourself to be subjected to.
- The body is a very intelligent mechanism that is always trying to keep in balance. Following a vegetarian, mostly alkaline

diet, with a balanced amount of protein, vegetables, fruits, whole grains, and very little carbohydrates is recommended for optimum personal health and the health of our planet.
- Society's present obsession with a meat-based diet is not sustainable by our planet and is the leading threat to our environment.
- Maintaining a daily exercise routine is essential for a lifetime of flexibility, strength, and energy. Find an activity you enjoy doing daily and which gives you a full exercise workout. Review the top twenty benefits of exercise to help you get started and stay on track.
- You have to learn how to identify stress and avoid it. High levels of stress can lead to a compromised immune system, increased sickness, and a shortened lifespan. Simple adjustments in our lifestyle can dramatically reduce the effects of stress.
- Meditation is the practice of stilling the mind and experiencing the peace and joy within. In this chapter, you discovered a step-by-step guide to a specific type of meditation developed by the author called Power Meditation. Power Meditation will do wonders for calming your mind and keeping your body healthy. It increases your vitality and rewards you with an immediate feeling of the energy of *sattva*.
- Certain types of music have a magical effect on mood, both triggering and enhancing positive feelings and reducing stress. Just as Hollywood producers are very particular about the soundtracks they apply to their movies, so should we be selective about the music we listen to in order to enhance our emotional state, relax, and reduce the effects of stress.

CHAPTER 4

Principle 2: Finding Your Purpose

*"There is only one corner of the universe
you can be certain of improving, and that's your own self."*
—Aldous Huxley

*"The winds of God are always blowing,
but you must set the sails."*
—Unknown

*"What we must decide is perhaps how we are valuable,
rather than how valuable we are."*
—Edgar Z. Friedenber

Loss of Purpose

IN HIS BOOK, *Drive: The Surprising Truth About What Motivates Us,* inspirational author, Daniel H. Pink, explains how the underlying operating system that propels our modern, capitalistic economy (and by association our very lives) actually deprives us of the most powerful motivator in life—PURPOSE.

This underlying operating system, which Pink calls Motivation 2.0, works according to the archaic and mostly redundant carrot-and-stick paradigm of motivating workers.

When people feel less and less purpose-driven, extreme activities begin to represent their expression of inner meaning and autonomy.

When we are absorbed in activities that align with our life purpose, however, we tend to feel happy and free from anxiety. In studies conducted over decades, it has been shown that when people enjoy their work, they report a state of mind that induces "optimal experience."[8]

Your Intrinsic Identity and Purpose

What is your purpose or intrinsic identity? How do you describe yourself? Do you say, "I am a doctor" or "I practice medicine"? Most people don't know clearly who they are.

Let us start with "occupation," for how we feel toward our work reflects how we feel about ourselves. Who we are is shaped by what we do, where we live, who our friends are, what we wear, what recreation we enjoy, and many other facets of our lives.

But to get a grip on who you are in truth, you need to understand yourself without the interference of who you were in the past, or the version of yourself which other people expect you to be. You have to discover what purpose in life makes you happy.

---

[8] Mihaly Csikszentmihaly, *Flow: The Psychology of Optimal Experience*, the classic work on how to achieve happiness (Harper Perennial Modern Classics, 2008), p. 39.

4 / Principle 2: Finding Your Purpose

Our preconceptions of who we are have been shaped by our education, the expectations of family, who we were up until now, our peers, and billions of dollars of media bombardment! It's not surprising that most people are a little confused about their real identity. This confusion makes us vulnerable to the vacillating nature of the mind. If you are not clear on who you are, this instability of the mind causes unhappiness and weakens your drive.

This instability causes dissatisfaction and reduces the richness of experience that is our birthright. The flickering instability of the mind repeats like a scratched record, or an endless pattern that distracts you from your identity and purpose.

In the ancient Sanskrit language, this intrinsic identity and purpose is called *dharma*.

Great Minds Think Alike

In our investigation of *dharma* it is interesting to note that great minds think alike. Paradigms devised by Hegel, Aristotle, Buddha, and the *Vedas*, have very similar conclusions. As the following table shows, each great thinker or school of philosophy has delineated a similar triad of external forces which influence us to act in ways which are more or less harmonious with our highest goals. They all seem to come to the same conclusion: acting

Source	Intense	Withdrawn	With Balance
Hegel	Thesis	Antithesis	Synthesis
Aristotle	Extreme	Deficit	Mean
Buddha	Materialistic	Asceticism	Middle Way
Vedas	*Rajas*	*Tamas*	*Sattva*

with balance leads to a more successful outcome than merely being swayed by productive or destructive impulses. So it is not only important to find our purpose but it is also important to pursue it with the correct attitude.

Discovering your Dharma

According to the *Vedas*, this triad of different approaches to intrinsic drive can be applied in all circumstances. I demonstrate this phenomenon in the table below. By extrapolating different aspects of our daily lives into these columns, you can decide for yourself which paradigm produces the best results.

Drive Factor	*Rajas* (Intense)	*Tamas* (Withdrawn)	*Sattva* (Balance)
Occupation	Career	Job	Vocation
Consciousness	Stressed	Depressed	Happy
Attitude	Hankering	Lamenting	Satisfied
Investment	Calculated risk—high return/loss	High risk—complete loss	Steady return with steady expansion

By studying the tables above, we can see that acting rationally, with mental balance in a state of *sattva* helps immensely in achieving vocational clarity, happiness, and inner satisfaction. Occupation (above) relates to our contribution to society. Do you see your occupation as your job, your career or your vocation?

When you see your personal contribution as a job, then it becomes merely an unpleasant activity you do to survive, because it pays the bills. If you see your daily participation in the external world as a career, you're doing it not only because it pays the bills, but also because you enjoy your work (in doses) and it offers you opportunities for growth. However, when you see your contribution as a vocation, you do it because you love it. You derive satisfaction from doing it no matter whether you are remunerated monetarily or not.

The Steps to Vocation:

- Discover your vocation in life.
  (See Guided Meditation for Vocational Clarity below)
- Make plans to begin engaging in that vocation and DON'T GIVE UP ON IT!
- Calm the mind as it struggles to try and force you to act and think according to old patterns and conditioning. (Use the *sattva* principles of balance, moderation and flexibility).
- Continue to practice *sattva* so that the mind will be brought under control to accept and assist you in pursuing your real purpose in life.

Once you have understood who you are or what your *dharma* is, it takes a lot of determination and effort to act according to your true nature, as the mind is set in its previous patterning. Successful people are those who engage in activities that they enjoy. If you're not enjoying your work, chances are you're not successful in terms of the depth of happiness you're experiencing. Pursuing your purpose will simultaneously make you feel happier while alleviating many anxieties and stresses in your life.

In this sublime state of balance, we free up psychic capital to empower our determination, confidence, focus, hope and depth of experience. Acting in *sattva* will empower you to break your bondage to the old patterning of the mind. This patterning has trapped most people on the roller coaster of dissatisfaction and confusion about their real purpose and identity.

To efficiently introduce a new way of living, you have to make changes both internally and externally. First transform your internal patterns of thinking, and then begin to adjust your external behaviors according to the new internal patterns.

> "The future makes way
> for the man who knows where he is going."
> —Ralph Waldo Emerson

> "The greatest thing in the world is not so much where we are,
> but in what direction we are moving."
> —Oliver Wendell Holmes

A Guided Meditation for Vocational Clarity

To help you gain clarity on finding your purpose and identity, I have developed a meditation that has helped many friends and colleagues find clarity of vocation. For best results, do this meditation in a peaceful location:

   1) Find a quiet place to sit, dim the lights and imagine that you have been given a large inheritance. The inheritance is so large that you can easily pay off your mortgage, give up your job, buy all the cars and other toys you have always desired, travel the world, invest millions in a retirement portfolio, and give generously to all the charities you love.

   2) Now, after you're done with your spending spree, ask yourself: "What is it that I really want to do with my life? What contribution would I most desire to make in this life that would increase

the happiness of myself and others?" (By asking this higher cognitive question, you stimulate the part of yourself that is most connected to your true purpose and identity. This question should be asked while you feel free of all the so-called pressures and responsibilities that are currently drawing on your energies. Don't limit yourself by your impressions of what people close to you would want from you, or even of who you are at present.)

3) When you get an answer, write it down explicitly. Now that you have the answer to the question of what you truly desire to contribute to society in this lifetime, imagine how happy it would make you. Imagine yourself actually in that role and begin to make it real for yourself. This vision of yourself is the picture in which you must invest your energy from now on! Become that person without worrying about any obstacles that may appear to obstruct you. Believe that you are that person.

Over time, this understanding of yourself will become more refined, but to begin the journey of self-discovery, simply start with your first impressions. Everything begins from subtle, in the form of thought, to concrete, in the form of everyday reality. The ingredient that solidifies what you conceive into what you can achieve is your psychic energy.

dharmam tu saksad bhagavat pranitam
(*Dharma* is your God-given gift.)[9]

It is very important to uncover your true nature. From a young age, many people carry a vibrant idea of who they are and what they want to achieve in life. Over time, their inner understanding

---

[9] *Bhagavata Purana* 6.3.19

fades away due to conditioning. In this meditation, try to evoke a childlike consciousness to get in touch with your real purpose and identity.

Your purpose and identity are a natural part of your personality that needs to be released into the world. Burying or holding back your true identity will cause depression, dissatisfaction, and many other negative emotions.

Fulfilling your purpose in life may not be easy at first, but endeavoring to follow your dreams will become the single most important source of happiness and peace of mind in your life. The fulfillment of positive, internal desires results in permanent improvements to the quality and quantity of our happiness and the happiness of those with whom we interact.

Just as the inherent nature of sugar is sweetness, the essence of fire is heat, and water cannot be separated from its wetness, so too do each of us have our inherent purpose or nature. According to the *Vedas*, an understanding of what constitutes the essential nature of all things is called *dharma*. The *dharma* of chili is that it is hot and the *dharma* of ice is that it is cold. Just as everything in the universe has its own special *dharma*, you too have your unique *dharma*.

According to the sages of the past, understanding your dharma and acting accordingly is the most important step for human success. Knowing one's life's purpose sets forth a sequence of events that leads to successful human existence.

This sequence is known as *dharma, artha, kama* and *moksha*. I have roughly translated these terms as follows:

4 / Principle 2: Finding Your Purpose

Know your nature and purpose	*dharma*
From *dharma* comes economic development	*artha*
From *artha* comes enjoyment	*kama*
After *kama* comes enlightenment	*moksha*

These ancient teachings emphasize the importance of *dharma*, because when we understand our *dharma* or purpose, *artha* or successful economic development follows like a shadow.

When we attain economic success, *kama* or enjoyment will follow naturally. From a state of satiated sensory enjoyment, we begin to seek greater truths and try to realize our spiritual nature—*moksha*.

Discovering Opportunities in Life

*"Opportunity dances with those
who are already on the dance floor."*
—H. Jackson Brown, Jr.

*"Opportunities are usually disguised as hard work,
so most people don't recognize them."*
—Ann Landers

Once we create a sphere of harmony around ourselves, free from anger and other negative emotions, it becomes easier to expand that balanced sphere outward towards the world. Your psychic energy can then be concentrated toward your purpose.

Being clear on your purpose allows perception to penetrate mental conditioning. The conditioning I'm talking about here is the type that interrupts your perception and gives rise to a running commentary in the mind which is counter-productive.

Knee-jerk reactive conditioning causes negative emotions to swell up for trivial things. For instance, if we hear that someone said something negative about us, we immediately tend to allow anger to pollute our consciousness. By challenging the beliefs that trigger this sort of unproductive anger, we can maintain our state of balance and mental equilibrium. When the chatter of mental conditioning and emotional turmoil disappears, our perception is focused on the now.

When we focus our consciousness on the present, a whole world of opportunities will begin to emerge.

Some people feel that opportunities only come around once in a lifetime or very rarely, but in reality, every moment is filled with opportunities. When we learn to bring our life into balance and live in the now, every moment is an opportunity at which to marvel. Like a child waking up on Easter morning to hunt for Easter eggs, we should be eager to discover the opportunities that every day brings.

It may be an opportunity to spend more time with a loved one, or an investment opportunity, or an opportunity to improve our health: whatever the opportunities are, we should become conscious of their presence and pursue them.

Pay Attention—Ask Questions

Being attentive to detail gives us access to discovering opportunities. The quality of our dealings in relationships, business and other areas is directly affected by the amount of attention we commit to them. Paying attention helps develop insight and understanding. Understanding or knowledge is the key to improvement, and improvement is the key to success. So how do we learn to pay attention? We have to stimulate our intelligence and focus. A good way to accomplish this is to interact with the subject, object or circumstance through asking questions about the subject or object, either of ourselves, of others or of the person with whom we are interacting.

To illustrate how powerful questions are, let's go back in history to the father of modern Western education, Socrates. Socrates developed a system of illuminating ideas called the Method of Elenchus, commonly known as the Socratic Method of Questioning. This method uses questions to test the veracity of statements or premises. By constantly questioning in the form of a dialectic, or dialogue between opposing views, a clearer understanding of truth can be achieved. Socrates established the first university in Athens called the Academy, where he applied these principles to enrich the different departments of knowledge taught there.

Another example of the power of questioning is found in ancient India. When Vyasadeva, the compiler of the *Vedas*, decided to summarize the *Vedas* into axiomatic truths, he wrote the *Vedanta Sutra,* which is comprised of 555 *sutras,* or condensed axioms. The first axiom in the *Vedanta Sutra* states, *atatho brahma jijnasa:* "Now that you have achieved a human form of life, you should ask questions to understand truth." We can see that in the great volumes of literary truths, the authors considered the concept of continual questioning as key to achieving success in all knowledge. Through questioning we uncover knowledge which gives us the opportunity to learn more and improve our mastery over a subject. To discover the hidden opportunity in something, we have to look closer and question from different angles of vision, or think outside the box. Questions are the tools that pry open the hidden opportunity cloaked beneath a set of conditions or circumstances.

Beware of Your Own "Opportunity Damper"

Many of us have developed an "opportunity damper" that filters out large amounts of information as irrelevant. This damper is a mental reflex that runs in automatic mode, a process that is technically called inhibitory modulation of sensual and cognitive stimuli. We have to learn how to flip off the mind's automatic switch to reverse the effects of this opportunity damper. Turning off our opportunity damper allows for clarity of perception. By a clear, correct perception of the world, and the information we receive from it, we learn how to analyze things from different angles of vision to find their salient quality of opportunity. Everything in existence has a purpose and is imbued with usefulness. Opportunity arises when undiscovered combinations of conditions, circumstances or objects become apparent to us.

By practicing *sattva*, the mind becomes a clear window between our intelligence and reality. This higher resolution of perception is only possible when we switch off the opportunity damper used by the mind to gray out reality. Acting on perceived opportunities will become natural to us and appear genius-like to others. We will even discover good opportunities within so-called bad circumstances or situations. Opportunities are available to everyone if they are willing to remove their self-imposed opportunity damper.

Distractions
When the mind is clogged with distractions our picture of reality is distorted.

By spending undivided, undistracted time with friends, family or business, we perceive each interaction with greater depth, unleashing an ocean of opportunities. Being in the now, not allowing our psychic bandwidth to be reduced by mental chatter, will allow us to see the beauty and greatness in everything and everyone.

With this kind of balanced observation, we develop a keen eye for opportunities and recognize negative aspects that should be avoided.

Perseverance, Consistency and Determination

When we discover an opportunity that is in alignment with our purpose and brings us closer to our goals for success, we should act immediately. Procrastinating or losing any opportunity to bring us closer to our goals erodes our self-confidence and determination.

The difference between successful people and losers is that a loser seldom acts on good ideas. A lot of people have good ideas and can see opportunities but only a successful person acts on them.

> "I always wanted to be somebody,
> but I should have been more specific."
> —Lily Tomlin

> "Opportunities are never lost.
> The other fellow takes those you miss."
> —Unknown

What distinguishes an achiever from a loser? It is perseverance, consistency and determination. What strengthens determination, consistency and perseverance? It is strengthened by focusing on the results of pursuing success, and understanding the consequences of not pursuing it.

Sattva is a state of mind that preserves psychic capital to nurture determination, consistency and perseverance which allows us to focus on the pursuit of success.

Discretion, the Better Part of Valor

When we understand our *dharma* we become clear about our personal, moral and ethical values. We have our own personally-prescribed moral code of living. How we truly examine and follow our own standards reflects how much we value ourselves. Did you ever get into a situation in which, due to peer pressure, you did something which you later regretted? Most of us can recall an instance in which we breached our own standards and, therefore, felt guilty. We should always aspire for higher standards.

Understanding ourselves, means that we know our boundaries clearly and protect and live by them fiercely.

If we fail to value our internal, moral compass, and the ethical values that make up who we are, we suffer internally and let ourselves down. By recapturing our purpose, we also regain a desire to raise our standards in all areas of life.

Discretion is a tool we should use more frequently. When you find yourself associating with people who have different standards than your own, using discretion will give you the ability to recognize the differences and enjoy their company without compromising your standards. Your standards are a part of your purpose and identity. Standards are different than beliefs, but beliefs and standards need to be in harmony with each other.

Why is it important to maintain your standards? Because breaking your standards disturbs your inner balance and drains your psychic capital. Like adaptogens or healing enzymes, your psychic

4 / Principle 2: Finding Your Purpose

reserve is constantly trying to restore mental equilibrium. Conserving this vital energy will enable you to use it for positive, constructive purposes.

Balancing Internal and External Goals

It is important to maintain a balance between external and internal goals. If we are simply hell-bent on getting as much as possible materially, without improving the quality of our character, we will lose our balance and set ourselves up for failure, greediness and miserliness. On the other hand, if we just try to improve internally without paying attention to our external situation, the imbalance could result in the scarcity mentality, reclusiveness, depression or emotional dryness. Balancing your desires to enjoy materially and improve internally is the solution; however, achieving these requires two different processes.

The Process for Fulfilling External Goals

1) Decide what you want.
2) Set out a plan to get it.
3) Empower your determination by magnifying your emotional state to attain it.
4) Offer that plan in the form of a seed of intention to the cosmic energy of Mother Nature.
4) Execute the plan attentively using psychic capital.
5) Use leverage, influence, perseverance, and intelligence to achieve it.
6) Attain it and offer thanks by doing something charitable.

The Process of Making Internal Changes

Upgrade your Internal Programs
With internal desires that require internal changes, the process works differently. Because our bodies and minds run on internal programs, which can be compared to software, it is important to:

- Upgrade your software or delete malfunctioning software.

Whatever your internal desire is, whether it is to become more charitable and compassionate or more loving to your family, you need to:

- Be ready to shift internal patterns of thinking.

Some of the internal patterns that you have are like harmful software that has no benefit and infect your consciousness while draining psychic capital.

- Delete or replace harmful software.

Upgrading Your Beliefs and Behaviors
If we want to improve our lives, we must desire not only to achieve material opulence, but also to attain an upgrade for our cognitive performance. By upgrading, we will reap the benefit of greater capabilities and better use of our time. It is essential that gaining material facilities should be balanced by internal improvement. Some behavioral patterns are positive and work well, while others may be outdated or faulty. It is important to:

- Slowly and systematically, begin to identify behaviors, habits or patterns that consistently cause emotional pain.

- Decide to change them.
- Be determined to replace them with balanced beliefs that generate a positive effect on your emotions, your body and other people.
- Become flexible and accept continual improvement in the way you think and act.
- Develop a willingness to adopt changes.

By considering the long-term effects of nurturing a desire to improve internally versus one to attain materially, you will invariably become motivated to increase happiness through internal change.

Since most people like to identify with the way they think now, their thinking becomes ossified.

The happiest people in the world are successful because they chose to become flexible by adopting beliefs that are balanced, and by improving and refining their existing beliefs.

Happiness and Purpose

Why have most people lost the hope that they can enjoy a vibrant, happy and successful life? The central reason is that they have allowed their life's purpose to be overshadowed by the mind and the influences of society. They have sacrificed their autonomy, and bought into the slavery of "work for reward."

Why does the mind—instead of directing you toward your real purpose and happiness—send you on a roller coaster of emotional uncertainty? The mind is dutifully trying to find happiness, but unfortunately it is working from an outdated rule book. This old paradigm implies that if you work hard—even though you don't like your work—you will put food on the table and afford the pleasures of life. Most of us are trained to sacrifice happiness by working in a job we dislike in order to gain money. This trend prioritizes sensual pleasure over inherent happiness. Inherent happiness is a natural state of contentment that a person can experience through meditation or self-awareness.

Our understanding of happiness directs our activities. Where do we derive our understanding of happiness from—the media, society, education or our role models? In order to achieve happiness, we need to be very clear about what happiness actually is. There is a discernible difference between sensual pleasure and internal bliss. If sensual pleasure created internal happiness, then money and a healthy body would be the currency of happiness. But experience tells us a different story. Many healthy and wealthy people are sorely depressed or highly stressed. Therefore, it is clear that internal happiness is not dependent on sensual satisfaction.

Scientific studies show that when people are offered incentive compensation in exchange for performance, they generally perform worse than those who are not offered such incentives. These findings seem to fly in the face of current business practices. The reason for this apparent contradiction is that people generally perform better by engaging in activities that give them a sense of purpose without being motivated by extrinsic rewards. In fact, studies have proven that such incentive rewards tend to decrease or limit performance![10]

We tend to limit ourselves with self-imposed conditions which have to be met before we allow ourselves to become happy. However, if we carefully analyze the self, we will realize that not only

---

[10]An experiment conducted by Gestalt psychologist Karl Duncker in the 1930s.

is the source of happiness within, but that it is boundless and limitless.

> "What do I need to be happy? God has given me the ability to be happy in my own situation simply by accepting what is present before me and doing the best I can with it. Can I not be content with this personal happiness? Do I need to get someone else's approval before my guilt and anxiety cease? Do I need to measure my happiness against my neighbor's (who may be across the planet) to be certain that I am indeed happy? Can happiness that's free, available to anyone anywhere and at any time, private and personal, be genuine? We are quite capable of being happy in the life He has provided for us, in which we can contentedly make our own ways, helped by His grace. We are ashamed to do so. For we need one thing more than happiness: we need approval. And the need for approval destroys our capacity for happiness." (Thomas Merton)

Four Reasons Successful People Are Happy

1) They have found their purpose and true identity in life, and are engaged in a meaningful vocation which they feel they could do forever.

2) They all maintain moral standards that are in line with their purpose.

3) They protect their standards and values, and give back to society.

4) Their activities are connected with constantly improving their service to other people.

A Quick Recap

- When we are absorbed in activities that align with our life's purpose, we tend to feel happy and free from anxiety.

- Why have most people lost the hope that they can enjoy a vibrant, happy, and successful life? The central reason for this phenomenon is that they have allowed their life's purpose to be colonized by the greater mind and the influences of society. Acting with purpose, in a state of mental balance, helps immensely in achieving vocational clarity, happiness, and inner satisfaction.
- The detailed guided meditation in this chapter assists you in discovering your true purpose and nature, which the *Vedas* call your *dharma*.
- Opportunities for improvement and success are available to everyone if they are willing to remove their self-imposed "opportunity damper." Once an opportunity that furthers your success or happiness is identified, act with conviction and determination.
- When we understand our *dharma* we become clear about our personal moral standards and ethical values. We learn how to balance our internal and external goals and how to "upgrade" our beliefs and behaviors.
- We tend to limit ourselves with self-imposed conditions which have to be met before we allow ourselves to become happy. However, if we carefully analyze the self, we realize that not only is it the source of happiness within, but that it is boundless and limitless.
- There are four reasons successful people are always happy. We should learn these and internalize them.

CHAPTER 5

Principle 3: Empowering Your Relationships

"Every act is either a call for love or an expression of love."
—Bhakti Tirtha Swami

"To love and be loved is to feel the sun from both sides."
—David Viscott, MD

"Nobody has ever measured, even the poets, how much a heart can hold."
—Cathy Morancy

Finding the Right Starting Point

TO HAVE TRUE meaningful relationships we need to learn how to resonate with others. So long as we remain affected by the mind's tendency to judge others and to discriminate because of their race, sex, appearance or social status we will not fully experience the true happiness of relationships in *sattva*. When we situate ourselves in *sattva* we see the consciousness within every living entity and meet their consciousness with ours. The understanding that all life is sacred will help to evolve our consciousness to a higher level.

Elusive Love

The word "love" brings to mind countless novels, plays, and movies which revolve around iconic heroes and heroines who seem to be engaged in a perpetual struggle to both elicit this emotion in others and express it satisfactorily themselves. Love is an intimate part of the human psyche, as integral as sweetness is to sugar and heat is to fire. Many of us express love often or yearn for it to imbue our every interaction.

Where does this love originate? Is it simply a genetic trait, an instinctive mechanism to ensure procreation, a mere weakness of human nature? Or is love the most endearing quality of our humanity? Where did it all begin? Are we becoming better at giving and receiving love, or worse? Do we really know how to capture it?

Through love, all hankering of the heart can be fulfilled. When we are in balance we can maintain and deepen our loving relationships with others. This chapter will help you to express your love appropriately to your children, significant other, friends and family. You will effortlessly win people over by resonating love. Most of all, this chapter will help to enhance your exchanges of care and affection in relationships with others.

Love is the underlying cause of abundance, wealth and happiness.

By digging deep into your heart to release the secrets of love and its application to the human spirit, you will understand yourself from the core. When you learn to apply love appropriately and ef-

5 / Principle 3: Empowering Your Relationships

fectively, you will begin to vibrate love outwardly. For those who have difficulty experiencing love, this chapter will be a gift. You will learn the secrets of giving and receiving love naturally. Love tends to be inherent rather than learned. This fact is easily perceivable in the relationships of children with their parents, and even animals with their young.

When we talk about having 'a broken heart' or 'feeling vacant', we cannot take a vitamin or pill to remedy the situation. If this were the case, such a supplement would be a blockbuster seller. Obviously, love is not dependent on any material formula. When conditions are right, love begins to blossom. Yet love comes from within, even though love is dependent on another person to evoke it. The presence of the object of love condenses and unleashes our internal happiness.

One of the distinguishing qualities of love is that it is an expression of our unique, total independence.

We are all independent and have the freedom to choose. This freedom of choice allows us to love or not to love. If love was instinctive, it would constitute an emotional prison, and would contradict the meaning of love. The aspect of choice, which allows you to choose whom to love, is unique to love's definition.

We have the potential for love deep in our hearts. Love seems to appear out of nowhere: it seems to be inborn, almost like a fire igniting from the dormant fuel in wood. How do we unlock it? How do we control it and harness it for all aspects of our existence? Love blossoms when we meet someone who evokes this dormant propensity. We experience a wonderful feeling in our hearts that lifts us on a cloud of dreams and passionate feelings. Love is so powerful that it can transform our lives, the lives of others and ultimately the world.

Love does not cost anything: it is a free resource inherent to all of us, yet it is more valuable than trillions of dollars. All we need is to excavate it and distribute it! The miraculous thing about love is the more you distribute, the more you receive.

As humans, we learn how to utilize energy resources expertly, either by mining deep into the earth to extract them or by harnessing the forces of nature. But how do we harness the greatest resource in life? The first step is to know what the resource is and how to locate it. Just as coal and oil are condensed forms of stored sunlight in the shape of mineralized rock and liquid, so too, love is a condensed form of internal spiritual energy. Just as we learn how to extract the energy from coal or oil for daily use, so too can love, in its variegated forms, power our lives when properly harnessed. But first, we have to gain a clearer understanding of the subject matter and to challenge any faulty beliefs that obscure our access to elevation in love.

Obstacles on the Path of Love

There are obstacles on the path of love, as many of us have experienced. We tend to guard our love vigilantly, and do not give it away easily. In this sense, we have to avoid being miserly with this part of ourselves. The fact that we protect our love is sometimes a boon and sometimes a mistake.

To guard our love from friends, family, a spouse or significant other is to starve ourselves and our close ones from the profound happiness found in the convergence of two powerful rivers of love.

Another obstacle is our need to be consistent or congruent. At times, we are reluctant to show affection because we would rather maintain a consistently neutral centerline than swing from love to disagreement. Neutrality is the borderline between negative emotions and positive emotions. By striving only for neutrality, one risks falling onto the negative side of the neutrality line where emotions like anger and others breed. Impartiality is one of the hardest barriers to break—it makes one impersonal, whereas being personal allows us to share our love.

Up Your Love Ante

Wouldn't it be wonderful to break the social paradigm of neutrality as our centerline emotion and instead establish higher forms of love as the norm on the playing field of life?

Upping the love ante does not necessarily mean an increase in external displays of affection, but rather getting in touch with your loving feelings.

There is a big difference between lust and love. Sometimes a man or women will profess their so-called love, but later it disappears. Lust is a bodily sexual need whereas true love is an emotional connection of the soul or spirit. Love develops through gradual stages and must not be mistaken for a sudden, passionate urge.

The heart is a gleaming, wonderfully bright orb that by nature beams endless love, but presently it is covered by opposing qualities and faulty beliefs. For anything that is tarnished, an agent exists that can easily reestablish the shine. What is the magic salve for the heart? As mentioned earlier, the object or person in whom we repose our love is a very powerful agent for reviving our heart's dormant love.

By applying your full psychic bandwidth in understanding someone else, you will begin to minimize the effects of this tarnished condition of the heart. When you associate with a person and commit all your attention to him or her, the beginning of a relationship is created. By sensitivity and boundless, loving affection, the desire to reciprocate is awakened in the heart.

Communication is the currency of a relationship and it should be exchanged equally to establish a harmonious relationship.

In personal relationships, it is important to be trusting and truthful. Truth means sharing our thoughts, feelings and needs with our partner. Successful relationships require a mood of surrender that allows us to inquire confidentially from our partner about his or her thoughts, feelings and needs. The "cold-shoulder treatment" has been the cause of many a dissatisfied spouse.

> *"So many catastrophes in love are only accidents of egotism."*
> —Hector Bianiciotti

Resolving Relationship Issues

In traditional Japanese culture, harmony or "wah" is essential. When there is a disturbance in wah, Japanese people immediately seek to reestablish it, for they specifically value harmony and balance in relationships. Interestingly, traditional Japanese couples frequently reestablish wah not through direct verbal communication, but rather through a symbolic reciprocation of loving behavior.

In general, there are two ways to resolve issues: either by direct communication or by positive behavior toward one another. Traditionally, the Japanese choose the latter as their method. In the culture of old Japan, if a couple found that the wah was broken,

5 / Principle 3: Empowering Your Relationships

they would go through a ritual to reestablish balance.

After a disagreement, the husband and wife would busy themselves with different activities that would help their minds to become peaceful. The husband would create a bouquet of flowers. He would take time to make the arrangement with artistic flair and subtle nuances, while reflecting on the wife's beauty and good qualities. While the husband focuses on his activity, the wife performs the ritual of making some flavorful tea. The key factor is her meditation on all the positive qualities of her husband during the performance of this ritual. After some time, both enter into a small room on the side of the house with doors so low it is necessary to bow to enter. Once in the room, they sit silently drinking the tea, while admiring the beauty of the flower arrangement on the table between them. In turn, they complement each other on the excellent quality of their creations. The process of ongoing positive reciprocation continues until the wah is reestablished.

*"Love is an unconditional commitment
to an imperfect person."*
—Unknown

*"A friend may be well reckoned
the masterpiece of nature."*
—Ralph Waldo Emerson

*"The supreme happiness of life
is the conviction that we are loved."*
—Victor Hugo

Relationships and Responsibility

The notion of responsibility constitutes a significant part of love, which is expressed primarily through providing necessities for one another. When someone loves you, he or she naturally wants to see you grow and have a healthy life. Therefore the act of providing, whether by cooking or by working to contribute money to the household, is a sign of love. If someone is not responsible, it is a sign of selfishness and a lack of love for you. This is the essential part of the relationship we call duty—a dutiful husband and wife provide for each other in their unique ways, or parents dutifully take care of their children in all respects.

To foster healthy relationships, it is important to engage in activities which generate new life.

A revival or strengthening of love, or what I call "wave peaks." is vital to create a steady increase in the quality of your love. Wave peaks are generated by the giving and receiving of gifts, such as a piece of jewelry or a surprise vacation. Wave peaks decorate the pattern of love with rich ornaments. Although gift-giving or spending special time together may seem like trivial activities, actually they constitute some of the most powerful methods of reinforcing and expanding loving relationships. This is a powerful way to show your gratitude toward those you care about.

If love has such a positive effect on ourselves and others, doesn't it make sense to try to spread as much caring as we can? The key to enriching our own experience of love lies in trying to give love to others. For most of us, a virtual wall exists in our mind that discriminates between those whom we should and should not love.

5 / Principle 3: Empowering Your Relationships

It is important to vibrate pure love from within, as this will attract loving people toward us. And vibrating pure love is the natural consequence of seeing all beings as intrinsically equal and connected to Mother Nature.

Generating a Vibration of Love

A lot of people yearn mostly for romantic love, but of course love can manifest in different ways according to circumstances. For instance, if your children are naughty, out of love, you may correct them. In this situation, love expresses itself through discipline. If we are to unleash this powerful force of love then we need to become aware more and more of how much we are holding it back. Generating a vibration of love will nourish compassion and concern for others, because we are blessed with the perception that everyone is related.

To develop these finer qualities of love, compassion, tolerance, sympathy and appreciation, we need to center ourselves within a universe of balance and concern for all. By so doing, we set no limits on accepting one another and sharing love with one another. As spoken in the Ten Commandments, "Love thy neighbor as thyself." Developing a good attitude towards others and good qualities within ourselves is the fertilizer that nourishes the lotus of love in our hearts.

"Service is the rent we pay for our room on earth."
—Lord Halifax

"One thing I do know: the only ones among you who will be really happy are those who have sought and found how to serve."
—Albert Schweitzer

Learning How to Resonate Love

Srila Rupa Goswami, a 16th-century Bengali saint and prolific author, categorized five varieties of relationships in his devotional work *Bhakti Rasamrita Sindhu*, (*The Ocean of Nectar of Divine Love*). This spiritual text educates and elevates the reader in explaining a process of mastery of the mind and senses. Srila Rupa Goswami taught that a sweet force known as *rasa*, or taste, drives our relationships.

Learning how to upgrade *rasa* is the subject of this chapter, a systematic approach to *bhakti*, or love. *Bhakti-rasa* means the drive for relationships that develop into pure love. Srila Rupa Goswami explains that upgrading our drive with devotion to the Divine, and seeing everyone as being connected to the Absolute Truth, is so powerful that it frees one from stress and anxiety and puts one in a permanent state of happiness.

Upgrading the quality of our love transforms all of our relationships to a lasting blissful experience of pure sattva.

Srila Rupa Goswami's lucid delineation of the anatomy of relationships is a great model for understanding the dynamics of human interaction.

Love is the sweetest level of a relationship. In life, we experience different varieties of relationships that are colored or imbued with different flavors and intensities of love. In this section we will look at Srila Rupa Goswami's categorization of relationships and their underlying qualities. By understanding the dynamics of these relationships, we can learn how to experience a greater depth of affection and care. When we learn how to exude these qualities we will automatically influence others to experience a higher level of interaction.

5 / Principle 3: Empowering Your Relationships

The Five Varieties of Loving Relationships

1) *Neutrality:* Love without familiarity.
2) *Servitude:* Love mixed with reverence, and slight familiarity.
3) *Friendship:* Love mixed with the feeling of equality and greater familiarity.
4) *Parenthood:* Love mixed with feelings of responsibility, nurturing, dependence and strong familiarity.
5) *Conjugal:* Romantic love filled with dependence and surrender.

Love becomes stronger in intensity as we move from one level to the next. Let's explore these five levels of relationships more clearly:

Neutrality

In a relationship of neutrality, we lovingly acknowledge the greatness of a powerful or famous person. While we accept his or her existence, we don't have any personal relationship or intimate knowledge of and association with such a personage.

Servitude

Servitude is what most people will experience in relation to their bosses, shareholders or board of directors if they happen to have a high esteem for them. The servitude paradigm automatically includes the element of neutrality or acceptance. In servitude there is a predominance of the mood of reverence, since familiarity is largely lacking in such relationships.

Friendship

In friendship, we find the element of sweetness and familiarity, and think of how we can please our friends emotionally. We endeavor to make them happy. Our relationship extends beyond the duty of the servant, to the urge to please our friend, because we want to attract his or her love toward us. Friendship encompasses all the qualities of neutrality and servitude, as well as more familiarity and equality.

Parental Affection or Mentorship

Parental affection has more closeness and dependence. This relationship is stronger than a friendship due to feelings that our loved one depends on us. Separation or termination of this relationship creates great pain to both parties. Parental affection includes all the elements of neutrality, servitude and friendship, while extending beyond them to encompass deep attachment and mentorship.

Conjugal or Nuptial Love

The most intimate relationship is conjugal love. In a relationship of conjugal love, we want to offer everything to our lover and exhibit complete dependence as well as let down all inhibitions. This relationship is sweetest when it is selfless. Conjugal love encompasses all the elements of neutrality, servitude, friendship and parental affection together with its own unique loveliness. In this type of relationship, we allow ourselves to dissolve all our internal barriers and surrender the full blossoming form of love to the beloved.

The Progression of Relationships

Aside from the variety of relationships that we may enjoy with our children, boss, parents or partner, we also vibrate a predominant mood toward the world. To clarify, even though relationships may

5 / Principle 3: Empowering Your Relationships

bring out various gradations of love, we exude an underlying vibration toward people we don't know (ranging from neutrality in most people, all the way up to love for advanced souls). This underlying attitude which we resonate helps to determine people's impression of us when they first meet us. I call this vibration the "centerline *rasa* of love."

For example, a young child surrounded and protected by family members may perceive strangers in the mood of neutrality. The child knows they exist but has no direct relationship with them. Therefore, the child's centerline vibration toward the world outside of family could be one of neutrality. Later when the child grows up, he or she begins to perceive teachers and other members of the community with an attitude of reverence (servitude). This respectful attitude is taught through social norms. The desire to please and show respect becomes the underlying centerline of their affection toward adults and people in general.

As the child grows into a teenager, he or she begins to see others with the potential for friendship mixed with reverence or servitude. Teenagers extend a vibration of camaraderie and begin to develop lasting friendships. At an advanced stage of evolution, the centerline attitude toward humanity may be a mood of paternal affection. This inspires one to do philanthropic work, such as feeding the poor and taking care of Mother Nature. People who predominantly exude paternal affection as their centerline rasa are attracted to the caring professions such as the clergy, medicine, or environmentalism.

The most intimate centerline rasa is the harmonious and unalloyed nature of the pure love experienced between two innocent lovers. This should not be misunderstood to be merely erotic attraction, but rather affection reflecting loving unison and mutual caring and appreciation.

Love is an unlimited source of psychic energy and can build our psychic reserve. By deepening our love, we are mining this potent reserve of psychic capital.

When we treat people in the world with deep loving feelings, our actions and words will always be pleasing. Such a mood of love toward the world is the symptom of abundance, and attracts success and happiness.

Loving feelings are a deep reserve of psychic capital because if we have affection even for our enemy, there is nothing our enemy can do to disturb our mental balance. It is negative feelings of hatred, anger, envy, and fear—especially fear—that causes us so much unhappiness. By mostly resonating love, we will remain unaffected by people who speak or act badly toward us. Love encompasses an overriding element of forgiveness. An everyday saying reflects the connection between affection and forgiveness: "Love means never having to say you're sorry." When we exude a positive loving mood as our centerline feeling toward the world, we simultaneously build more and more psychic capital. The most powerful, inherent emotion we have is love. It protects us from negative emotions and makes difficult things become easy.

Creating a Peaceful Space

Any incongruity in relationships bothers us both consciously and subconsciously, taking its toll by draining our conscious energy. Most of us are familiar with the saying: "Charity begins at home."

Our first priority is to take an interest in everyone in our circle of friends and family by spending quality time improving our relationships and encouraging people around us.

5 / Principle 3: Empowering Your Relationships

By so doing, we will notice that our own mind becomes more peaceful. Focusing our consciousness on simple interactions with the people around us transforms our perception and makes us sensitive to others. Notice what motivates people and what makes them feel good about themselves. Boosting the confidence and determination of friends and family members nurtures relationships and is conducive for happiness. It is very important to create a peaceful space in your life where you are able to foster happiness and love. Having a powerful, balanced base in your world from which you expand your influence is integral to achieving success.

Attentive and Effective Communication

> *"There is no greater loan than a sympathetic ear."*
> —Frank Tyger

Accurately verbalizing our thoughts and feelings makes us unique as a species. Sometimes, however, even though we may possess a sophisticated vocabulary and consider ourselves socially broad-minded, miscommunication may nevertheless wreak devastating consequences in our lives. Many people suffer from depression or suppression because they are misunderstood, or lack communication skills. Understanding another person is the first step to attentive communication.

We have been blessed with two ears and one mouth. Therefore, it is good practice to listen twice as much as we speak.

Errors in Communication

> *"The less you talk, the more you're listened to."*
> —Abigail van Buren

> "The most important thing in communication
> is to hear what isn't being said."
> —Peter F. Drucker

Even though you may be very expert at communication yourself, if your spouse or friends lack communication skills, life can be a real challenge. Most often people find it hard to express what is really bothering them and begin to "act up." Acting up, or passive-aggressive behavior, normally confuses the situation more and leaves the other side fumbling to decipher the real cause of unhappiness. Therefore, it is always a good practice to have clear communication skills. A central part of clear communication is to transmit an unambiguous message to the person with whom you are relating. If you want to communicate approval or disapproval for something they said or did, clarity and directness is always more effective than silence, acting up, or beating around the bush.

Jumping the Gun

Another major error in communication is to think you know what others are thinking, or what their motivations are. By making assumptions, we allow our faulty beliefs to obscure our perception of others' actions. By interpreting and judging others, we end up exposing our own faults. To overcome a tendency to jump to conclusions, verify first what you think others may be feeling or doing by asking them directly in a compassionate way. By doing this, we can be certain that the messages we are receiving are being interpreted accurately by us. Once we are clear about the communication, try to empathize and not criticize or judge. By empathizing, we begin to understand other persons' needs.

Mirroring for Clarity

When you are communicating with a person about his or her feelings, it is always good practice to repeat in your own words what you think you had understood from what was said. This gives the person the opportunity to verify whether he or she has conveyed his or her true feelings to you accurately and also may prompt further revelations he or she may want to verbalize.

Listening and verifying will ensure that no wires get crossed, just as in the airline industry, where pilots are required to repeat all instructions they receive from air traffic control back to the control tower.

After clearly understanding the other party, question further or clearly state your feelings or comments. Be sure to articulate exactly what you mean by being congruent. You can ask the person if they understood you just to verify you're both still on the same page. Once you have successfully executed the steps of listening, verifying and questioning appropriately, communicate to others in such a way that they leave the conversation feeling that there has been a meeting of the minds.

Communicating to Empower Others

There are many tools presented in this book and at our seminars that can be used to enhance communication through *sattva*. The objective of *sattva* is to magnify or empower the positive emotions of the people with whom you are communicating. Think of a scale of 1–10, 1 representing apathy or depression and 10 representing bliss and *sattva*. To communicate effectively, we have to understand where someone is placed on this scale so that we can strategically elevate their mood.

Again, attentive communication does not merely involve understanding the words others articulate, but also their position on the scale in terms of happiness. Once you can assess where they are on this scale and understand clearly what they are saying, you can communicate so as to uplift their mood. It is important to uplift their mood while conversing.

You can uplift someone's mood by:
1) Paying compliments.
2) Slightly changing the tone of your voice.
3) Helping them to break a painful pattern that is playing out in their heads by replacing it with a pleasant one.
4) And ALWAYS remember to at least treat others the way you would have others treat you.

Verifying what someone is saying clearly, and understanding their mood or emotions will evoke in them the feeling that they can trust you and that you care. If you're practicing *sattva*, besides uplifting others, you should learn to communicate with persons who uplift you when you are down. It is good to have a list of friends in your personal phonebook who motivate you positively. If you're feeling unmotivated try contacting friends who uplift you even though you may not feel like it. Most of the time, they will assist in shifting your mood in a positive way.

A Quick Recap

- Developing a clearer understanding of the origin and impetus of love allows you to excavate your heart and give love openly, without reservation. Love is the underlying cause of abundance, wealth, and happiness.
- We need to be mindful of the obstacles on the path of love and

5 / Principle 3: Empowering Your Relationships

learn how to resolve relationship issues. An integral aspect of healthy relationships is responsibility and duty.
- This chapter explores the five levels of love, a force of concentrated, psychic energy which becomes stronger in intensity as we move from one level to the next. At the highest level of loving exchange, we unleash unconditional love, which resonates outward to create a relationship of pure harmony and coexistence with all living beings.
- When we treat people in the world with deep loving feelings, our actions and words will always be pleasing. Such a mood of love toward the world is the symptom of abundance and attracts success and happiness.
- Learning attentive and effective communication is essential for building positive relationships. Be careful to mirror what is being said—don't "jump the gun." Communicate in such a way that you empower others with your words.

CHAPTER 6

Principle 4: Sattva Clarity— Removing Inner Roadblocks

IN THIS CHAPTER you will find many useful tools to help overcome some of the most daunting roadblocks on your journey to a successful, happy life. You may read through the entire chapter all at once, or you may decide to read one of the topics per day and implement it into your daily program of improvement. These tools require some practical implementation into your mindset to yield permanent benefit. Nobody likes to take out the trash, but it is a necessary labor to maintain a healthy existence.

Dispelling Negative Core Beliefs

> *"By bringing the mind into* sattva, *one understands the self. When one understands the self, cheerfulness, focus of mind, sense control and contentment is achieved. From this the highest happiness is attained."*
>
> —Patanjali's *Yoga Sutras* II. 41–42

> *"It's hard to defeat an enemy who has an outpost in your own head."*
> —Sally Compton

When attempting to synchronize your outer self to reflect your true inner self, you will inevitably face misconceptions and negative conditioning which cause the mind to act according to faulty patterns. To break free from such patterning of the mind requires powerful tools.

There are two ways to change the faulty patterns of the mind: one is to change behavior and the other is to alter the belief that powers a particular pattern, or set of patterns.

Negative core beliefs influence the way in which we perceive and interpret our experiences and are counter-productive and self-defeating. These beliefs can be likened to templates that affect the way we view ourselves and others. Negative beliefs such as "I am unattractive," "everyone is superior to me," "something horrible is going to happen," or "people are thinking badly about me" are often the cause for unhappy feelings. Such distorted thinking makes us react to and perceive situations in distorted ways.

If such thinking persists, it causes depression, lack of self-esteem, anxiety, and other problems. In this section, I aim to help you recognize when your thoughts arise from a faulty belief, and to show you how to challenge that belief. This process will empower you to become more flexible and balanced.

Real Life Examples

By recognizing faulty beliefs, we can reframe them into a *sattvic* or balanced way of thinking. Reframing beliefs neutralizes the negative results of wrong thinking. I will now share some real-life examples of negative thinking and positive reframing with you.

Tim and Sylvia were arguing a lot. At one time, it seemed as if things would fall apart. They attended marriage counseling a few months ago and hardly argue at all now. Whenever they do argue, though, Sylvia immediately thinks their relationship is finished and the counseling was useless!

This is an example of someone whose beliefs drive her to think in terms of black-and-white. Black-and-white thinking programs a person to expect that either a situation should be perfect, or that the situation is terrible and won't work at all. In order for Sylvia to stop herself from overreacting, she needs to challenge and adjust her core faulty belief. Sylvia needs to see that there are shades of gray between black and white, and that nothing in the world is perfect. If Sylvia adjusts her thinking in this way, she will not get so depressed and angry over small imperfections in her relationships.

When we observe negative feelings or behavior in ourselves and others, it is important for us to uncover the faulty belief that drives them.

Another example:

Dave is a very organized and punctual businessman. He believes that he should never be late for any appointment. Due to this belief, he is overcome by anxiety while he rushes through the busy traffic on his way to an appointment. His belief causes him to feel intense, inner stress even though he can't change the fact that the traffic is congested.

Later that evening, Dave takes his wife Susan to the supermarket. As he is feeling tired from rushing to appointments all day, he decides to stay in the car. Before Susan gets out of the car, Dave asks her how long she will be in the supermarket, and Susan replies that she will be about ten minutes. After twenty-five minutes, Dave becomes furious and frustrated, feeling that Susan is disrespecting him and wasting his time. When Susan arrives, she is shocked to see David fuming with anger because she took fifteen minutes more than he expected.

If Dave can adjust his belief in order to accept that not everything will go according to plan—and that you have to be flexible and resourceful when it doesn't—then he won't feel stress, anxiety, and anger nearly as often as he does now. There are many beliefs that we hold onto that are self-defeating. Whenever you feel bad or find yourself behaving in a negative way, analyze the situation to uncover the faulty belief that is supporting this behavior or uncomfortable emotion.

Here is a practical model for altering the pattern of such faulty core beliefs, based on the work of Albert Ellis (1913–2007), an acclaimed American cognitive-behavioral psychologist:

1) Situation (the situation that triggers a reaction)
2) Belief (the underlying negative or faulty belief)
3) Reaction (the resultant negative feelings or behavior)
4) Challenge faulty belief, reframe into balanced belief
5) Get better result and conserve your psychic capital

The key point is to challenge the faulty beliefs and find a balanced approach that more accurately defines reality. The best way to do that is to challenge the underlying premise behind a particular faulty belief.

Dave's Faulty Belief

I must be punctual all the time, and everyone around me must also be punctual and have the same values I do.

The Logical Challenge

David could reason with himself as follows:

"Being punctual all the time is impossible because so many factors are out of my control. Why get so disturbed when at most, if I'm late, it's only a few minutes? Usually if I'm a few minutes late, people understand. People have the right to hold different values from mine. Therefore, it follows that if I hold them up to my standards, there is a good possibility they may fall short because their standards may differ from mine. It makes sense to conclude that it is better to be flexible when dealing with other people." These are just some of the logical challenges that David could use on himself to break the faulty belief that caused him to experience unnecessary anger, anxiety and relationship stress.

Breaking the Cycle with a Different Behavior

While David can challenge his faulty beliefs through analytical logic, he can also break the negative cycle by behaving differently. For example, he has the option to call his clients to let them know that he was running a little late for the appointment. Most people will be understanding and tell him not to worry. When David's wife was taking longer than she had anticipated at the store, David could have taken the opportunity either to review his schedule for the next day, or to snooze in the car, or to call his wife on her cell phone to see if everything was okay, or to call a friend on the phone and have a friendly chat. David could also have decided to relax and listen to his favorite music. There are many activities we can do to help break the cycles created by faulty beliefs.

Catastrophizing

What we will notice is that our faulty core beliefs always cause people to overreact. We become emotionally charged because our unspoken rules are being broken. By exaggerating the negative consequences of a situation, we feel far greater stress than is appropriate. Instead of "catastrophizing" minor issues by faulty perception, try challenging your faulty beliefs and replacing them with balanced beliefs. When we have so many faulty rules by which we live, eventually someone will come along and interrupt our peace by breaking them, therefore it is better not to be disturbed by others' actions. By being exemplary ourselves we will teach others how to act appropriately.

Here are ten examples of faulty beliefs that often hold people back from being a success and feeling happy:

1) My life should be easy and free of problems.
2) I must be loved by everyone.
3) It's better to avoid problems than to confront them.
4) If I make a mistake, I am stupid, a failure and an idiot.
5) The world is full of danger, so it's better to stay at home.
6) I have never been successful so why even try?
7) The world owes me a living.
8) Those who don't share my beliefs are evil.
9) People I don't like are bad and should be punished.
10) Everyone is looking at me.

Sometimes we don't realize that we hold a faulty belief, or set of beliefs, but catch ourselves behaving in ways that are negative or disturbing to others. When we scrutinize the cause of this irrational behavior, we find that inevitably it started with a faulty belief. Therefore, we should monitor our behavior and challenge the underlying beliefs that cause such self-sabotaging behavior.

If you focus on the goal of conserving your psychic energy and experiencing happiness while helping others to become happy, it will be very easy to begin to re-pattern your thoughts.

6 / Principle 4: Sattva Clarity

Try to focus on the benefits of changing your thinking patterns. You should also remember the consequences of not changing faulty beliefs and irrational thinking patterns. These re-patterning tools (introspective logic and different behavioral choices) act as the code with which you can rewrite the new program by which your mind will become balanced and peaceful.

Changing Behavior to Strengthen New Patterns

The process of changing your behavior will strengthen and empower your resolve to change your thinking and vice versa. Therefore, it is good to create a plan to improve your life on all fronts. First of all, list all the items you want to change and improve in your life. Maybe you're feeling guilty about neglecting your health? Put it on the list! Here are some areas for improvement that you may want to place on your personal list: Health, Vocation, Relationships, Spirituality, Community, and Environment.

Life is made up of a sequence of days. If you can get one day in balance, or sattva, *and then repeat it, you will automatically create a balanced, powerful and happy life. Start with one day.*

Try to get up early and do a little exercise. How you begin your day sets the tempo and rhythm for the whole day. For instance, I do one hour of Hatha Yoga in the morning. This immediately puts my body and mind into balance. Even if you're not so good at yoga or exercise, start slowly with fifteen minutes and gradually improve and increase daily. While doing your exercise, try to absorb yourself in the activity without allowing the mind to surge into the future or dwell in the past. Be present in the activity. Don't try to block out any stretching pain in your tendons or body, just experience your exercise. After breakfast, schedule your time to cover as much as possible of your list of areas to improve, and goals that will put you in line with your true purpose.

During the day, remember that if you start feeling any negative emotions, it's usually because you're not challenging faulty beliefs and are being reactive instead of proactive. Remember that all the negative emotions simply burn up your vital and precious, psychic capital. Start seeing these negative emotions as thieves who are plundering your successful future. Begin to recognize patterns that cause you stress.

Overcoming the Dreaded Commute

When I lived in Carlsbad, Southern California, the commute to work every day caused me a lot of undue stress. Though I tried hard to relax, I found myself struggling to maintain momentum and equilibrium in the midst of delays and agitated drivers. I decided to change my behavior to strengthen new patterns and find a quieter route. I was happily surprised to discover a beautiful scenic back road from Carlsbad to Escondido. This route was one of winding roads and rolling hills—and most importantly, no agitated drivers and very few traffic lights. After driving this route for months, I had to take the freeway one day due to bush fires. I was happily surprised that I no longer felt agitated, but rather felt very relaxed and peaceful listening to my favorite music even though traffic conditions were terrible. Here is an example where I changed my actions which caused my behavior to change giving me a better result.

Altering those environmental or internal factors that cause you stress or anxiety is very important to conserving your psychic capital. Try to experience the beauty in everything. When speaking to friends or business associates keep conversations positive and upbeat and don't allow your mind to dwell on negativity.

When you begin to develop eyes like a bee seeking honey and nectar instead of eyes like a fly attracted to dirt and open wounds, your resolution and depth of experience will begin to return.

Proper time management is a very important factor in constructing a daily routine. Utilize your time wisely for investing in the variety of life. It is also important to rest when needed. Little power naps can give the body and mind the rest they need. Constantly monitor your reactions and stop 'catastrophizing' minor annoyances. Laughing helps to empower your state, so do it often. Avoid excessive alcohol, carbohydrates, caffeine and fatty foods. Recognize what you can control and don't fret about those things you can't.

In the evening, invest some time in celebrating the goals you've achieved that day. Go over the improvements you've already made, and then ask yourself what you can do to improve and succeed tomorrow. Make sure you get a good night's rest.

> "This uncontrolled mind is the greatest enemy of the living entity. If one gives it a chance, it will grow more and more powerful and will become victorious."
> —Srimad Bhagavatam 5.11.17

> "The mind is restless, turbulent, obstinate, and very strong, O Krishna, and to subdue it, I think, is more difficult than controlling the wind."
> —Bhagavad Gita 6.34

Ignoring the Mind

A common mistake we make is to become impatient: we want change and success now! However, success comes from regulation and improving consistently. Let's become like the rising moon, not like a shooting star. Commit to a regimen of daily reducing negative emotions, and keeping mental balance in *sattva*. Daily channel your psychic energy with determination to succeed in your vocation and other aspects of life.

The best way to deal with a turbulent mind is to ignore it! There is a lot of truth to this statement.

You could spend many hours trying to analyze the reasons for your problems, but your time is better utilized by asking how you can improve your situation. Great life-transformational and motivational speakers like Anthony Robbins, Deepak Chopra, and Wayne Dyer achieve great success by reinforcing positive activities in their daily lives.

One of the tools we should develop is the ability to ignore the mind's unhealthy tendency to "binge out" on negativity and instead engage in positive alternatives.

In his *Yoga Sutras,* the great yogi and author, Patanjali, talks about how the mind both dilutes and discolors consciousness. The essence of yoga is to become focused on positivity and ignore the distractions that the mind may present.

The key is to train the mind to achieve success even if we think success is out of reach. Napoleon Hill, one of the pioneers in personal-success literature, said: "If you can conceive it, you can achieve it." All human success starts with a dream, and in achieving that dream, we find success.

> *"Tension is who you think you should be.
> Relaxation is who you are."*
>
> —Chinese proverb

Constant Improvement: The RASIC System

Anthony Robbins has developed a system called CANI, which stands for Constant And Never-Ending Improvement. I regard Robbins' system, which I have adapted to form RASIC (Regulated And Steady Improvement Consistently), as one of the keys to success—because it works. In Sanskrit, *rasic* means a concentrated, blissful attitude. By following a daily pattern of regular and steady improvement, consistently, we can naturally acquire a blissful attitude. RASIC helps the mind achieve concurrent mental stability and momentum toward purpose-driven success.

The principle of constant improvement, or RASIC, is so powerful that it has been implemented in corporate culture for decades. In Japan, companies like Toyota implement systems such as Kaizen or HoshinKanri at Hewlett Packard. On a daily basis we should make a list of different areas of our life that we should improve. For example we may want to improve our exercise program, our diet, relationships, our impact on the environment, economic situation, or our mood, etc. By daily reviewing the list we will begin to make tangible life-long improvements that will impact the quality of our life.

Asking the Right Questions

Why do these processes work? How is it that Japan, which was a nation that produced below-standard products before World War II, became a powerhouse of successful industry? These principles work because questions are constantly asked about how to improve the system. If we ask the right questions, we get better answers than if we never ask any questions.

A few weeks ago, I was in the car with my family, when my oldest daughter said, "Hey Dad, why don't we go to the beach today?" Since I had been working on this chapter of the book, I responded, "Well, I could think of many reasons why we can't go to the beach today. Why don't you pose the question in a positive way?" Whatever questions we ask ourselves will elicit a particular kind of answer. Therefore, if we are always asking "Why can't I become rich?" our minds will naturally search for unlimited reasons why we can't become rich. The key is to ask "How can I become rich?", or "What if I took a particular action, wouldn't that be great?"

It is very important to phrase our questions correctly to ourselves.

If we continually work toward our goals while asking positively charged questions, we will see that success will be waiting at our door.

Releasing Self-Judgment

One of the greatest factors impeding success and happiness is self-judgment. Just as we dig deep to lay the foundation for a strong building, throwing out all the sand and rubble, similarly we have to remove the dirt of self-judgment from the depths of our consciousness. Self-judgment holds us back, triggers low self-esteem, causes depression and magnifies problems rather than solutions. This also minimizes our ability to think abundantly.

The Two Sources of Self-Judgment

There are many reasons for this problem. They can be divided into two categories: internal and external. When we are affected by external influences, something outside of our control has reinforced these negative feelings. An abusive parent who continually tells a child that he or she is useless and good for nothing is an example of an external influence. Eventually, the child begins to believe these statements, and develops an inferiority complex. Another example of an external influence is social conditioning that dictates that we be a certain weight or wear certain clothes.

External Factors that Influence Self-Esteem
1) Childhood Experiences—Abusive parents, denigrating or labeling as useless.
2) Personality Traits—Anxious tendency, compulsively focusing on the negative.
3) Feedback from Others—Negative feedback from a partner or colleagues.
4) Social Conditioning—Faulty beliefs about appearance, educational achievements, etc.

The internal factors that influence us to feel unworthy or judge ourselves are usually based on faulty beliefs. If you are harboring a belief that is not very flexible, it is a belief that should be challenged in order for you to overcome its influence on your self-esteem. The first stage of removing self-judgment and low self-esteem is to recognize where the problem is coming from, and then to challenge the faulty belief that supports it.

Internal Thinking That Influences Self-Esteem
1) Focusing on Mistakes or Failures in the Past—"I dropped out of college, my whole life is a failure."
2) Black-and-White—"If I'm not the best at what I do, then I'm useless."
3) Comparing—"My best friends are slim and beautiful, I'm depressed."

4) Need for Constant Approval—"My husband didn't compliment me today, I'm getting old and useless."

Concentrate on the Present

Let's concentrate on positive activities that strengthen self-esteem and remove any tendency for self-judgment. It is important to see each new day as a great new opportunity that is not affected or reduced by the past. Most of our negative conditioning and judgments involve acts of punishing and penalizing ourselves for activities that have dissolved into the past. Mental self-flagellation is a confirmation that we don't believe we can ever change.

> *"A bad habit never disappears miraculously.*
> *It's an undo-it-yourself project."*
> —Abigail van Buren

> *"Forget the past, it sleeps, and neither*
> *the future dream at all, act in times that are with thee,*
> *and progress ye shall call."*
> —Bhaktivinoda Thakura, Bengali saint

> *"I'm an old man who has known a great many problems,*
> *most of which never happened."*
> —Mark Twain

Positive Steps You Can Take

Not only should we not judge ourselves on the past, but we should also refrain from making judgments on aspects of ourselves or our lives that we can't change, such as the color of our skin, height, our parents or our children. These attributes are part of us, and we have to be accepting that we are who we are because of, or despite, any such permanent aspects of ourselves.

In your morning meditation, picture yourself as pure and uncontaminated by the past. Try not to think too much about the future. Allowing the mind to dwell on the past or future will simply waste your energy, especially during meditation. Envision yourself as a fresh new creation ready to explore the opportunities of a brand new day. Keep in mind that you have been blessed with a fresh new start, unaffected by everything that has happened in the past. Try to get in touch with the present, feel life, breathe life and experience life. As the rising of the sun's rays bring to life the color and form of a new day, so too let your consciousness connect directly with your reality.

If you live with someone who has a tendency to criticize or suppress you, tell them how such hurtful words make you feel, but don't react to them negatively. Keep all such negative internal or external words or thoughts away from you, and maintain the peace and calm of the beauty of life and living. Focus your mind on the new day and the wonderful opportunities that it has given you.

Remember this is your life. It is a gift that you own.

Although people can try to influence you, no one controls your mind except you. You need to take full responsibility for driving that mind with thoughts of your purpose and the meaning that you seek from life. Don't allow negative thoughts to take over valuable psychic and emotional real estate.

Every moment is precious and a valuable gift: there are no refunds on time.

The only process that can insure your present and constant happiness and success is upgrading your thinking. Improving your lifestyle while neglecting to upgrade your mind will never satisfy you. The way we think is like a habit, and it is difficult to change without practice. Therefore, centering yourself in thoughts of the 'now' will easily allow you to begin to change the processes of thought that hold you back.

Becoming more focused will help you channel the time and psychic energy needed to challenge any faulty beliefs that you may be harboring. Spend the time analyzing and neutralizing the judgments you have about yourself and others. Becoming free from negative judgments will allow you to expand your confidence in yourself and those around you.

The Most Devastating of All Emotions

"Keep your mouth shut when you are swimming and when you are angry."

—Unknown

"If you are patient in one moment of anger, you will escape a hundred days of sorrow."

—Chinese epigram

You may have experienced trying to concentrate during a business meeting, but failed to do so because your mind was stuck on an argument you had with someone close to you. To avoid such situations, one must realize that anger is the most devastating of all emotions in terms of consumption of psychic capital.

Anger not only consumes your consciousness, but it also blinds your intelligence.

6 / Principle 4: Sattva Clarity

Anger frequently arises when we are interrupted in some way or other or our plans are frustrated. By replaying past scenarios either mentally or verbally, we can feed anger. Time is divided into past, present and future. We should be living in the present, not dwelling on the past, or thinking about the future while we are engaged in important activities. It is appropriate to think of the future when we are planning and strategizing, but not very good when we are having dinner with our loved ones, or a meaningful conversation with a friend.

The reactive mind tends to get very annoyed when its processes are interrupted, such as when someone cuts you off on the freeway, or a person is rude to you. Now that you have been disturbed, are you going to allow the circumstances to burn up all your remaining psychic capital and simultaneously punish yourself by suspending your happy state? Hopefully not!

Try to see anger as an emotion that should only be used for protecting the innocent and yourself from mortal danger.

Healthy anger is a powerful transformation of psychic energy into physical power for the purpose of warding off danger. If we allow ourselves to switch on anger but fail to use that energy positively, it has a negative effect on our body and mind. Not only does it pollute the body and mind, it also takes hours and sometimes days for the negative effect to dissipate.

Ending the Tendency to Criticize

> "Two things are bad for the heart—
> running upstairs and running down people."
> —Unknown

An ancient saying advises that "a thief thinks the whole world is full of thieves." The tendency to judge others is a reflection on the way we see ourselves. When you criticize others, imagine that the same negative qualities you perceive are becoming your own through the act of criticizing. If you can visualize this effectively, you will succeed in reducing critical thoughts. Once you can stop judging others, automatically you will stop judging yourself.

Every person is a valuable touchstone of precious condensed life. As everyone has unlimited potential, we should train ourselves daily to try to see the potential in others.

By endeavoring to find the divine spark in others, we become more qualified to see the spark of eternal joy within ourselves, and fan it into a great flame. Recognizing the potential in others and fanning the spark of their greatness will empower you unlimitedly. The consciousness of abundance will empower your mindstream, and the more you empower and value others, the more you will be empowered and valued.

Removing self-judgment toward yourself becomes easier when your stop judging others. Increasing your own self-esteem becomes easier when you empower others to grow their self-esteem.

Mastery means the more you see the value in others, the more you tap into your own value, resources and strength. Self-mastery is difficult for those who are gazing through the glasses of judgment.

Protect Your Positive State of Mind

> "The most handicapped person
> in the world is a negative thinker."
> —Unknown

6 / Principle 4: Sattva Clarity

> *"The person who is wrapped up in himself is generally overdressed."*
>
> —Unknown

Have you ever been excited about an idea and told someone how you intended to achieve it? Can you remember how you felt when that person shot down your idea? Not very excited any more, right? Success is born from the concentration of ideas and the determination to achieve them. If people feed your negativity at the embryonic stage of an idea, their influence will dilute your determination and enthusiasm. Therefore, besides patterning your mind to be positive, you need to use the tool of discretion to avoid those people who continually make negative statements and shoot down your dreams.

The end result of maintaining relationships with negative people is that you will drain your psychic capital and become emotionally weak.

Such association results in low self-esteem, and eventually even depression. When you take away people's dreams, they lose their purpose. When purpose is lost, they resort to intoxication, excess eating or sex as a way to replace happiness with sensual pleasure. Excess in these activities becomes very destructive to the internal balance of the mind and body: subsequently, their depth of happiness becomes more and more shallow. Remember to guard yourself fiercely against negative influences. Remember that part of your identity is to uphold your standards. By regularly and steadily improving your standards, you will be able to avoid bad association and seek out the positive association of people who give you confidence, and support your determination to achieve your goals.

If you want to become happy and successful more often in relationships and life, try to follow these nine key steps on a daily basis:

1) Become aware of your faulty beliefs.

2) Be determined to challenge all faulty beliefs that lead to negative emotions or negative behavior.

3) Reframe your beliefs to be balanced and realistic.

4) Change your behavior to challenge negative emotional states.

5) Practice RASIC: Regulated And Steady Improvement Consistently.

6) Ask yourself at least five positively-framed questions on how you can improve the key areas of your life daily.

7) Develop momentum by adding balanced variety to your day.

8) Improve your health through exercise and diet.

9) Fiercely avoid negative influences.

Overcoming Your "Immunity to Change"

With so much emphasis on acquiring technical skills in modern Western societies, is it possible that we have neglected the development of another set of essential skills, ones which could assist greatly in satisfying our need to find happiness and live harmoniously as a group? Improving our mental capacity and consciousness is something that should be ongoing. How we learn to perceive the world should bring us closer to being happier individually and collectively. Even as recently as the 1980s, scientists believed that an adult's mental progress plateaued after adolescence.

Recent developments in science and education project a different picture, for what we know now is that the possibility of upgrading consciousness even after adolescence is not merely theoretical. Scientists are currently exploring the field of neuroplasticity, which encompasses the possibility that the human brain has the ability to change physically as a result of one's experience no matter what one's age. I support the view that this potential adaptability and expansion results from personal, progressive shifts of consciousness upward.

Adaptive Thinking Verses Linear Thinking

The Industrial Revolution and the Age of Enlightenment geared education in the First World and elsewhere to prepare students only for economic productivity through linear thinking rather than adaptive thinking. Linear thinking works well when we are dealing with objects or a production line, whereas adaptive thinking works well when relating to and motivating people, and with ever-changing and complex systems. Due to universal education, there have been great leaps in medicine and technology that benefited society through better facilities and standards of living. However, since we are living in an increasingly "post-linear" age, where both work and social spaces are progressively dynamic and unpredictable, we must change our strategies in education and move toward a more adaptive paradigm. Unless we do so, we will deprive people of the most important tool: learning how to adapt or change. The ability to change our thinking is a simple process when it is taught and practiced, but extremely difficult for someone unfamiliar with it.

Imagine hypothetically that you looked through a red-colored lens all your life. In such a situation, you would naturally accept that the world is made up of different shades of red. If someone were to distance the lens from your eyes, you would suddenly see the full spectrum of colors on the periphery. This shift in perspective would alter the way you understood your perception. You would now understand that it was the lens that was creating your inaccurate perception, and not reality itself. Similarly, when we remove ourselves from our subjective view of the world and see it with an objective perspective, a multifaceted clarity begins to come into focus. This type of shift in perspective causes an adaptive change to the way we think.

Like a caterpillar that has developed wings, our whole frame of reference changes and we discover a new and beautiful world, full of opportunities and fresh life.

The technique of removing the subjective aberrations that cloud our perception can sometimes be a difficult process. The reason for this is that we are attached to our perceptions. We identify them as being part of us. To be told to alter our perceptions or adjust them may seem like an attack on us. When we incorporate our perceptions, understandings and beliefs into a rigid, almost physical idea of who we are, those perceptions become part of our greater "body." Just as the physical body has an immune system that fends off any attack, similarly we have a kind of psychological defense system that resists changes.

Harvard professors in Adult Learning, Robert Kegan and Lisa Lahey, term this phenomenon "immunity to change."[11] After more than thirty years of research, Kegan and Lahey discovered that our immunity to change is intimately connected to our faulty beliefs or big assumptions, and that if we are unable to alter those beliefs and assumptions, then change is not possible. In order for change to occur, we have to see our underlying beliefs and assumptions clearly with objective vision and then begin

---

[11] Robert Kegan and Lisa Laskow Lahey, *Immunity to Change: How to Overcome It and Unlock the Potential in Yourself and Your Organization* (Boston, MA: Harvard Business, 2009).

to grow ourselves bigger, like the caterpillar transforming into a butterfly.

> *"You must want to fly so much that you are willing to give up being a caterpillar."*
> —Trina Paulus

This concept of "getting bigger" is part of Harvard Professor, Ronald A. Heifetz's seminal work on adaptive leadership. By helping people face challenges through improving their adaptive ability, Heifetz guides them out of the fuzziness of their own subjective viewpoint to a higher vision. In his book *Leadership Without Easy Answers* (1994), Heifetz shows how a leader could potentially transform his or her notion of leadership from "influencing the community to follow the leader's vision" to "influencing the community to face its problems."[12] Those leaders who shift their consciousness upward will begin to influence others to solve problems through non-coercive means.

In their decades of research, Kegan and Lahey developed what they call an Immunity X-Ray, a soul-searching device that outlines a possible mental map of opposing forces that disable our determination to change. These kinds of tools are very powerful in uncovering explicitly the faulty beliefs and assumptions that cause us to maintain habits and attitudes diametrically opposite to ones we aspire to have. To illustrate how these tools work, I have included an example of an "Immunity X-Ray Map" (see tables on following pages).

In the first table you will notice that Greg has written in column 1 a single "Big Goal" that he has identified for improvement.

---

[12] Heifetz, *Leadership Without Easy Answers,* 14–15.

The "Big Assumptions" in column 4 of the second table cause Greg to act out negatively and do things he in fact does not like or want to do. Columns 3 and 4 represent ways of thinking to which Greg is habituated. The counterproductive result of such thinking can be seen in column 2. If Greg can grow himself bigger and adapt like the caterpillar, seeing no more use in the subtle assumptions and commitments in columns 3 and 4 to which he is currently attached, then Greg will be able to elevate himself and flit like a butterfly toward his objective in column 1.

By structuring an X-Ray chart like this for yourself, it becomes easy to discover the hidden commitments and assumptions you make that are counterproductive to the changes you always wish and hope to achieve. While the previous section addresses your faulty beliefs and challenges you to replace them with more flex-

1. Commitment (Improvement Goal)	2. Doing/Not Doing Instead
To be a better husband (being more sensitive, showing affection, making her feel great about herself, taking an interest in her hobbies and pursuits)	Absorbed in my personal life too much Not attentive to her interests Schedule my time around my plans and daily activities When she complains, become defensive instead of attentive When she gives advice, I generally override it or take it with a pinch of salt

ible and balanced ones, this section will enable you to learn not only how to address your faulty beliefs, but also how to uncover the hidden competing commitments that you have made to yourself that perhaps are no longer useful. With this knowledge, you will be empowered to apply a more elevated approach of thinking to achieving your goals. People find the X-Ray session at our seminars to be very helpful and empowering.

If you really want to go beyond wishful thinking and dreaming, and escape from lack of determination and congruency, then you have to address your problems with adaptive changes rather than technical ones.

3. Hidden Competing Commitments	4. Big Assumptions
To not want to seem too hen-pecked	That I am the most important person in our lives and my attention should be limited to advancing the financial aspect
Maybe I will compromise my masculinity	
She should be more attentive to my needs than her own	That being attentive and sensitive is not a manly quality
She may take advantage of my kindness to her and become more demanding	That I will become bored with an interaction about my wife's interests. I assume that my wife has no experience and therefore cannot offer good advice

The ability to separate our personal perceptions, assumptions and agenda from a situation constitutes not just a good tool for leadership but a great tool for challenging the faulty beliefs and stumbling blocks that obstruct our own need to change.

The Strength of Faulty Assumptions

For example, if you want to lose fifteen pounds of weight, you could change your diet by eliminating certain foods. However, merely changing your diet does not address any of the issues that cause you to over-eat in the first place. By addressing the hidden assumptions and subconscious commitments that are creating this immunity to change, you will be able to create an adaptive lifestyle, change more successfully and with less of a struggle.

It is only when you can break down this immunity to change that you can change.

The culturally dominant faulty belief is that by effecting a technical change or solution, we solve the problem. Unfortunately, it is only when we endeavor for an adaptive change that we are able to effect permanent change and adopt habits and behaviors that we sincerely desire.

There is a high cost to our immunity to change. Kegan and Lahey cite the following example: "Not long ago, a medical study showed that if heart doctors tell their seriously at-risk heart patients they will literally die if they do not make changes to their personal lives—diet, exercise, smoking—still only one in seven is actually able to make the changes."[13] Even though the six hypothetically doomed patients all want to live long lives, their faulty

---

[13] Kegan and Lahey, *Immunity to Change*, 1.

6 / Principle 4: Sattva Clarity

assumptions and hidden competing commitments create a devastating immunity to change. If they were able to reframe their assumptions and counterproductive commitments internally, they would greatly increase their chances of survival. In summary, we must change our cognitions to change our behavior.

To make a paradigm shift, we have to learn how to perceive our lives objectively through practice, practice and more practice of adaptive thinking.

Why not create your own Immunity X-Ray Map? Begin to transform your life upward by pursuing your purpose. Experience a more vibrant connection with reality. By living in *sattva,* or in the "now," many problems begin to dissolve because the chattering of the mind and the internal mechanisms that execute that chatter are switched off. The tools mentioned in this section will help you dismantle the internal mechanisms that obstruct you from succeeding in your purpose, goals, relationships and happiness.

By taking the time to create your own Immunity X-Ray Map, you will come in touch with the aspects of yourself that are working against your success and happiness. You will be equipped with a new, more adaptive mindset to dismantle the mechanisms that are stopping you from moving forward. Learn to understand the benefits of changing for the better, as change becomes scary when you don't understand all the steps. By introspectively challenging your faulty beliefs, you will disable the fear that stops you from activating the change you need.

Remember, by implementing successful, adaptive changes in your life, you will be able to power-up to the next expansion of consciousness. As you gain more control over your destiny and your mind, you will begin to enter into the state of *sattva* and realize that you have transformed positively. It is this adaptive upgrade to your perception that allows you to comfortably and smoothly embrace changes that will empower your success.

Once the process of disabling your faulty beliefs and hidden commitments becomes second nature you can begin to enter into the meditative state called sattva.

Striving to Consume or Improve?

We live in an age in which we find ourselves dependent on fossil fuels for all aspects of life. This dependency has changed the paradigm for most humans from striving to improve to striving to consume. When we get in touch with and connect to the hidden power of nature, our creativity and enthusiasm come alive again. By tapping into your *sattva* state, you will observe nature's powerful creative ability to nurture and manifest all desires. Some people are conscious of it, while others are not. By practice, these metaphysical laws will become more and more real for you. Eventually you will realize that the old adage that you have to be careful what you wish for is actually true. One practical way to get in touch with nature is to go hiking, mountain climbing, sailing, etc. When we reintegrate our consciousness into natural environments there is an immediate powerful effect nature has on the way we think and feel. Spending quality time outdoors will help balance your understanding of the organic natural cycle of life. A person that experiences his natural inherent happiness is doing so by a deep rooted realization of his connection to nature.

A Quick Recap

- When attempting to synchronize your outer self to reflect your true inner self you will inevitably face misconceptions and negative conditioning which cause the mind to act according

6 / Principle 4: Sattva Clarity

to faulty patterns. The two ways to change the faulty patterns of the mind are described in detail in this chapter: change your behavior and alter your beliefs.

- You explore two real-life examples of negative thinking and then the positive reframing for each one. Ten common, faulty core beliefs are listed along with the five steps for altering them.
- We give you some tips on how to change negative behaviors on a daily basis.
- How to train the mind by ignoring it, and following the RASIC system for steadily improving your life, is described in detail.
- The internal and external sources of self-judgment are explained along with the positive steps to become free from this crippling roadblock.
- Learn to end the tendency to criticize by seeing the value and potential in others and avoid anger at all cost.
- Protect your positive state of mind by being careful who you associate with. Nine key steps are delineated, which if followed on a daily basis, lead to increased happiness and success in your life and relationships.
- Learn how to overcome your immunity to change by adaptive thinking. You are introduced to the "Immunity X-Ray," a soul-searching device that outlines a possible mental map of opposing forces that disable your determination to change. To illustrate how these tools work, a detailed example of an Immunity X-Ray Map is included. Construct your own Immunity X-Ray Map in order to break down unconscious resistance to change and attain your dreams.
- Spending time outdoors will help balance your understanding of the organic, natural cycle of life. A person who experiences his natural inherent happiness is doing so by a deep-rooted realization of his connection to nature.

CHAPTER 7

Principle 5: Abundance Mindset

"As the purse is emptied, the heart is filled."
—Victor Hugo

"Nothing teaches character better than generosity."
—Jim Rohn

Think in Terms of Abundance

BY LIVING WITH a scarcity mentality, we tend to evaluate our lives in terms of the things we don't have. Focusing our psychic energy toward what we lack in life makes us consistently dissatisfied.

When you see somebody else's success, you may imagine that this has depleted the universal pot of success and that the chances of your own success are reduced. This mentality breeds miserliness, envy, and depression. It stunts your determination to succeed.

Those who harbor a scarcity belief prefer to remain in debt. They are worried that "if I pay my debt down, I will not be able to get the things I need and want. I have to keep as much as I can and give as little as possible." Those with an abundance mindset believe that by giving they will not become losers but they will become better people.

When you develop the eyes of abundance, you see that everyone has access to all the resources available.

If you feel you are burdened with the scarcity mentality, try thinking in terms of abundance. The unlimited ocean of resources and happiness available in your world will then come clearly into focus in your mind's eye. We begin by removing the faulty conception that "I will never be successful." Everyone has freedom to harness opportunity and share in success. Become convinced that you have the tools and determination to succeed. Adjust your beliefs to "I will take the opportunities that lead to success with determination," and "Success will come to me by doing the things I have always dreamed to do," and "I enjoy the activities I do in the process of developing my dreams."

Once you have changed your beliefs, the next step is to take action. Changing your behavior is critical to applying any changed cognitions. Begin to make plans for executing activities toward your goals. Sometimes you may think that you lack the money, connections, or talent, or you may conjure up any number of excuses why you can't succeed. Even though you may not know where in the world things are going to come from, don't let not knowing bother you. Just put it out there.

The secret to abundance is "ask and you shall receive." If you don't ask, you won't receive.

Mother Nature is dynamic. One of her secrets is that she plays an active role in helping her dependents fulfill their desires. We can

7 / Principle 5: Abundance Mindset

see the essential role of nature in an activity as basic as baking bread. When we bake bread, first we make the dough and then it is set aside so that the yeast can take effect by making the dough rise. At the right time, we put the dough in the oven, which is set at a specific temperature. We wait for a defined amount of time to pass before the loaf is baked. Even though the baker is endeavoring in various ways, nature contributes by fueling the interaction of the dough with the yeast over time, and the interaction of the dough with the heat of the oven. At the right moment, the bread is baked, and we get to enjoy a hot, fragrant loaf.

The baker is not passive: he acts and Mother Nature acts also. An altered vision will enable us to perceive the huge potential energy and resources in the world, and by the combination of our effort and help from Mother Nature, we will achieve success. If you can conceive it, you can achieve it, because Mother Nature is an incubator for your desires. The secret is that once you put a thought out into the cosmic psychic pool, the cosmic psychic energy begins to nurture it. If you tend to the seed you have planted, very soon it will begin to have a life of its own.

Nurturing and Weeding

With the mentality of abundance, you can begin to plant many seeds and nurture them with the help of nature. The more you plan and prepare a seed, the more it is likely to fructify into the creation you envision. Planned in detail, your goals and ambitions are creating the blueprints or DNA for your creation. The cosmic pool of psychic energy begins to breathe life into your dreams and ambitions. The more psychic capital you commit to your desires, ambitions and goals, the quicker they fructify.

This process is a way of compressing time. Things grow in time, but growth can be sped up by nurturing with the proper ingredients. The super-growth steroid for success is your psychic capital. How much can you commit to it?

Again, it is important to avoid negative emotions, negative association, and negative behavior. They deplete your psychic capital and drain the life out of your goals and ambitions.

We can see how adopting the belief of abundance is far superior to the belief in scarcity. Successful, joyous people are those who believe in abundance and give back in reciprocation for all the gifts they have received.

Challenging the underlying faulty belief in scarcity is the first step to changing your circumstances. As previously mentioned, when you focus on scarcity, your perception of your life is in terms of what you don't have. In abundance, you have firm faith that whatever you can conceive, you can achieve.

The simple secrets of abundance:
1) Pursue your dreams.
2) Make a detailed plan or blueprint.
3) Offer that plan or blueprint to Mother Nature.
4) Tend to your creation as it begins to come to life.
5) Share your creation and give back.

Abundance and Opening Your Heart

> "With malice toward none; with charity for all."
> —Abraham Lincoln

How do we tap into the abundance that the world constantly offers us? The consciousness of abundance is the opposite of the consciousness of scarcity. Abundance is a positive state of mind

7 / Principle 5: Abundance Mindset

that must be developed if you want to become successful.

Many people who are afflicted with miserliness or the "scarcity mentality" never feel satisfied with what they have, and therefore, even though objectively they may be very wealthy, they never give in charity. The abundant-minded person, even though he or she may possess very little, always feels wealthy and therefore loves to help those who are helpless and less fortunate than he or she is.

If you want to be wealthy, you must enjoy giving in charity. If you want to be wise, then learn how to listen. If you want to be a good leader, become a good follower. If you want to be strong, protect the weak. If you want to be enthusiastic, then encourage and compliment others.

When giving is in balance with receiving, an uncanny phenomenon occurs. Those who give a lot find that they always receive more in return, so giving never depletes but actually replenishes. There are many loving exchanges we can share; of which giving is a very powerful one. It shows others that we care and that the world cares. When we retain a miserly attitude, we only punish ourselves.

By being miserly, we lose the feeling that anything is possible. We feel the world is a hard place where everything we get is ours through our own hard work, a feeling due to excessive attachment for the fruits of our labor. Abundant-minded people feel that the world is taking care of them, and therefore it is their duty to give back no matter how modest their resources. It is a sign of gratitude for all the blessings that they constantly feel privileged to receive.

Developing abundance removes a damaging, faulty belief that impedes our success. That faulty belief can be phrased as "whatever I receive belongs to me, so I shouldn't have to share, even if I accumulate more than I need," as well as "accumulating things in this world will make me happy." We have to challenge these faulty beliefs by seeing that they are self-defeating. Therefore, we must adjust our thinking to align with an abundant mindset.

When we think that happiness comes from owning or accumulating things in this world, we set ourselves up for disappointment.

> "A man is rich in proportion to
> the number of things he can afford to let alone."
> —Henry David Thoreau

People, Not Things, Bring True Happiness

We live in a world with objects and people. We should use things and value people, not use people and value things. Our happiness comes from interacting with this world, and especially the people in it. When we place more value on the objects in this world and disregard the people in it, we become unhappy. When we put value on people, we become willing to give up some of the objects under our trust to make others happy. Becoming attached to the fruits of work—being miserly—is self-defeating.

When we practice abundance, we immediately realize that we receive more than we give.

The more we try to give, the more abundant nature is willing to entrust to us. For example, recently The Bill & Melinda Gates Foundation have allocated approximately $35 billion to an endowment fund for charitable activities. This Foundation is committed to enhance healthcare globally and reduce extreme poverty, as well as to expand educational opportunities. In 2006, American industrialist and philanthropist Warren Buffett, pledged around $30 billion toward the foundation. Microsoft also pledges to match charitable contributions of its employees up to $20,000 per person per annum. Frequently, the richest people in the world are the ones who give the most and most often.

> *"No person was ever honored for what he received. Honor has been the reward for what he gave."*
> —Calvin Coolidge

> *"The fragrance always stays in the hand that gives a rose."*
> —Hada Bejar

Universal Abundance

Supporting those in need can be as simple as volunteering our time. Or if we are blessed with success and wealth, donating to charities opens our heart to others. Most people express their happiness when they are with their friends, associates and family. How do we experience our inner joy with those whom we don't know, or with whom we are barely acquainted?

The best way to share our bliss with others is by giving to our community in different ways. When our heart begins to unlock towards others, we set into motion a powerful dynamic of reciprocation.

We begin to see our network as not just friends, family and associates, but everyone in our community and the world. The environment, together with its various life forms, becomes an integral part of our network. With this abundant perception, we will begin to develop the desire to protect and support our extended network.

An abundant-minded person doesn't dwell on acquiring more money. Rather, abundant-minded people have faith in the reciprocal nature of the universe and know without a doubt that all their desires will be fulfilled. By balancing the desire to be wealthy or successful with the desire to give in charity or to volunteer your time, you will always receive more than your needs. The more you give others, the more you will receive in return. Opening your heart to giving triggers your inner happiness to manifest.

By giving, we balance our success with charity and our happiness with making others happy.

When we incorporate community, environment and the planet into our personal network, we generate positive emotions toward them. These positive emotions are necessary because we all live on the same planet and should take responsibility for her protection and the well-being of the earth's population.

Try not to think of what you are giving, but try to think of what you are holding back. Share some of your time and realizations with others. Sometimes this kind of sharing can "mentor in" a realization that changes another's life! Just remember that if you love the world, how much love can you personally give? Conversely, if the world loves you, how much of that abundant love can you handle? We are very small and can only give and love on our limited scale, but when our community or planet recognizes and loves us, what an abundance of love and giving do we stand to receive!

Abundance is a key quality of successfully minded people. Successful people have core beliefs that are not one-sided, and help them to see things as they are. We have to practice changing our core beliefs or conditionings in order to nurture abundance. Abundance will open our hearts to experience the happiness of reciprocation with humanity, the environment and Nature herself.

7 / Principle 5: Abundance Mindset

If you want to know how you treat yourself inside, then take a look at how you treat others on the outside. With mastery, all purposes are served at once. Self-mastery is not an artificial show of external confidence, but rather the genuine result of truly valuing life.

Overall if we strive for abundance and learn to appreciate how valuable our life is, we will begin to live in the abundance of the universe. In this way we become harmonious with Nature.

Six principles of abundance that open your heart:
1) If you share more, you receive more.
2) When you give to the world with two hands, the world gives back to you with millions of hands.
3) Give back before you become successful.
4) Scarcity mentality channels your consciousness toward what you don't have, creating constant dissatisfaction, fear and low self-esteem.
5) The scarcity mindset puts you in competition with the whole world.
6) The abundance mindset puts you in harmony with the entire universe.

A Quick Recap

- Successful, joyous people are those who believe in abundance and give back in reciprocation for all the gifts they have received.
- In abundance, we have firm faith that whatever we can conceive, we can achieve.
- It is important that the goals we set for ourselves are in balance. We need to change our beliefs and our behaviors, avoid negative emotions and association. Internalize the five simple secrets of abundance.

- If we want to be wealthy, we must enjoy giving in charity. If we want to be wise, then learn how to listen. If we want to be a good leader, become a good follower. If we want to be strong, protect the weak. If we want to be enthusiastic, then encourage and compliment others.
- Learn how to use things and value people instead of using people and valuing things.
- The best way to share our bliss with others is by giving to our community in different ways. When our heart begins to unlock towards others, we set into motion a powerful dynamic of reciprocation.
- Internalize the six principles that open your heart to abundance.

CHAPTER 8

Principle 6: Being in the Present

"Yesterday's the past, tomorrow's the future, and today is a gift. That's why they call it the present."
—Unknown

"Your vision will become clear only when you can look into your own heart. Who looks outside, dreams; who looks inside, awakens."
—Carl Jung

The "Bliss" of High-Risk Behavior

A WORLD-FAMOUS BASE JUMPER and extreme sportsman back-flips off the edge of a gigantic cliff in Norway. Dressed in a wing suit, Jeb Corliss appears to catch the wind beneath the webbing spanning his arms and legs, and, like a humanoid squirrel, he guides his flight along the contours of the mammoth rock face at over a hundred miles per hour.

This sport is so thrilling that the participants go out of their way to "proximity fly," that is to fall closer and closer to the jagged cliffs and mountain's edge until they can almost touch it. Just a few hundred feet before hitting the ground, he opens his parachute. Elated, Jeb Corliss reaches the ground safely. This is not how it always ends. In 2012 Jeb smashed into the side of Table Mountain after a more than 200-foot drop, breaking both his legs.

"When I pop out into the open air and get that first look at how far away the ground is, time stops, it gets really quiet, I hear birds chirping, I drift around in my own thoughts—all in a nanosecond," says professional skier Julian Carr of front flipping off a 60-foot cliff at Utah's Alta ski resort. Carr loves launching himself off cliffs on skis so much that he holds two world records in the sport.[14]

Have you ever wondered what makes people become addicted to high-risk activities? Such unusual happiness is only experienced when our sensual, mental or intellectual stimuli are freed from the noise of our mind. Extreme sporting activities automatically switch off unnecessary mental chatter and enable the participant to commit full psychic bandwidth to the activity, and induce psychic clarity. By full "psychic bandwidth" I refer here to committing the entire spectrum of mental energy available, the potential of which many of us have not realized yet.

"Psychic clarity" can be defined as an altered state of unusual depth and lucidity, a "beingness," which, though frequently perceived as extraordinary, is in fact our natural birthright.

Looking in the Wrong Places

Similarly some people turn to drugs or become adrenalin junk-

---

[14] Link from National Geographic website.http://adventure.national geographic.com/adventure/extreme-photo-of-the-week/?source=email _adventure#/lulian-carr-alta-utah_36951_600x450.jpg

8 / Principle 6: Being in the Present

ies; some have extramarital affairs; and others even physically or emotionally hurt themselves. Why does it take such extreme measures for people to break free from the mental weather pattern that obstructs their pure consciousness? Have the normal activities of life become so dull and banal that people are forced to participate in extreme sports or high-risk activities? As we look back on the last hundred years or so in the West, we notice that our culture has changed to encompass greater risk, violence, and extreme behaviors. Narcotics have become the number one means for teenagers to experience a heightened sense of reality. Prescription drugs and alcohol are frequently used to break down the inhibitions or mental walls that stop people from enjoying peak experience.

These kinds of extreme behaviors are attempts to fulfill the need to "be there," or participate in life with the highest amount of attention, to really 'be one' with the experience of it.

Being one with the moment, or perceiving our external reality with unobstructed, riveted attention, allows us to experience life with our direct consciousness. That is to say, without interference from the turbulent mind. The methods mentioned above can temporarily assist us in achieving these experiences—but at a price: either by dumbing down our minds through intoxicants, or by invoking very palpably the fear of death by high-risk sports.

There is no doubt that heightened perception is definitely a desirable platform from which to perceive reality. So why don't we experience this depth of reality on a regular basis? One reason is that our consciousness is usually scattered. We are generally distracted from our immediate, direct perception. Most people are engaged in jobs and activities they don't enjoy, which give very little purpose to their lives. Therefore their minds are always distracted, trying desperately to find meaning and happiness, but never quite attaining it. Because most people don't know how to switch off the mind when appropriate, they do extreme activities to force the mind into the background. Learning how to control the mind will allow one access to the on/off switch of the mind at any time. One of the biggest obstacles on the path to happiness is to allow the mind to discolor all of your experiences.

Getting into the "Zone" or Sattva

When you find yourself experiencing stress, anxiety, anger or any of the negative emotions, the most important step to take is to know that your consciousness is being negatively affected and be clear on what to do next. Whenever I feel the onset of any of these emotions for whatever reason, I relax and change gears so to speak. Switching from a negative emotional state to a positive state is almost like changing gears. It is an immediate change and requires the switching of priorities in the mind. I expand my mind to see the bigger picture—a type of zooming out that allows my positive nature to inhabit my presence. When we are experiencing negative emotions it constricts our presence around the negative emotions. Learn how to expand your consciousness to be populated by the giants of positive feelings. This practice will become second nature to a point where it is no longer a conscious flipping of a switch but rather a peaceful transition.

The recent field of positive psychology pioneered by the Hungarian psychologist and thinker, Mihaly Csikszentmihalyi, in his book *Flow: The Psychology of Optimal Experience* has given rise to practical techniques that will help you unlock the secrets of human happiness, motivation and self-realization. For the layman, psychic energy is the energy that observes, directs, experi-

8 / Principle 6: Being in the Present

ences and expresses. Our mind is the faculty that focuses psychic energy, concentrates it and directs it in terms of the past, present or future. Psychic energy is depleted by anxiety, stress, depression and other negative emotions. Controlled correctly, this current of consciousness becomes the vehicle for fulfilling your purpose. It is the key to achieving happiness and a greater depth of experience.

How we use this psychic energy or psychic bandwidth determines how much attention we are able to commit to a given task. Csikszentmihalyi explains how the process of committing our full bandwidth of psychic energy to a particular moment or series of moments can produce an "optimal experience," which he terms—you guessed it—"flow." This experience of fully focused psychic energy is sometimes called "being in the zone."[15]

Those who are able to get into the "zone" or "flow" most often are people who are able to become deeply absorbed in activities which they find very satisfying, such as a surgeon performing a four-hour operation or a violinist playing their favorite Beethoven concerto. These feelings of absorption and happiness are felt most consistently by those who engage in activities that align well with their vocational purpose in life.

Understanding the Flow of Consciousness

Consciousness is a complex mechanism, which through proper understanding and training, can be expanded. In order to expand consciousness, we have to be willing to upgrade our way of being rather than thinking.

---

[15] Mihaly Csikszentmihaly, *Flow: The Psychology of Optimal Experience*, the classic work on how to achieve happiness (Harper Perennial Modern Classics, 2008), p. 39.

First of all, we have to understand the anatomy of consciousness and the mechanisms that calibrate it, focus it, scatter it, and shift it between moods.

When we perceive things with the mind as our center of gravity—the mind will tend to label our perceptions as favorable or unfavorable. In balanced perception, we allow consciousness seated in the intelligence to flow unobstructed toward the objects of perception. With this balance the process of scrutiny and judgment of the mind is withdrawn. When we perceive our environment with intelligence, free from mental chatter, we gain appreciation and real knowledge of our perceptions. This is how we begin to be in the present.

Perception without mental chatter brings happiness through appreciation and real knowledge.

It is also very important *not* to allow the past or future to initiate dialog with your perception of the present. Being in the now produces clear perception without the mental interference of hankering for things in the future or lamenting about difficulties in the past.

Just as an automobile changes its gears as it goes faster, similarly when consciousness is upgraded, it expands. When people are locked into the sensual platform, their consciousness becomes limited to very instinctive behavior, like the consciousness of animals. Animals are stuck in a limited consciousness that allows them access to their senses and the world around them coupled with limited instinctive reactive choices. If we now shift consciousness up a gear, we will arrive on the mental platform, which is where humans have an advantage. The human being has the ability to analyze his environment, while his choices are elevated

8 / Principle 6: Being in the Present

by the faculty of the mind. If we can learn to shift our consciousness out of the limits of the senses and the mind, we will reach the intellectual platform.

The intellectual platform allows humans to change their lifestyle, create paradigm shifts, invent and develop, amongst other skills. The intellectual platform still uses the mind as an intermediary reference and therefore is still locked into the sphere of the external creation. To reach the higher stage of *sattva*, a person has to elevate his consciousness beyond the intellect and direct it deep into the heart. It is through the opening of the lotus petals of the heart, currently protecting our real consciousness within, that we genuinely connect with our innermost self, which is imbued with pure love, absolute, full *sattva* and true knowledge. This is the secret of being in the present.

For example, when meeting someone for the first time, the mind works hard to figure out whether this person is a friend or a foe. This constant chatter of the mind could distract from developing rapport or from remembering his or her name! To properly interact with someone, we have to consciously turn off this chatter before we can develop a balanced opinion or gain real knowledge about him or her. Or in other words, we should give respect by dedicating an undivided flow of consciousness toward our interactions with others. A lot of people use alcohol or drugs to dumb down the mind and switch off its inhibitions and constant chatter. However, these artificial means of mind control do not last long, while the damaging side effects tend to neutralize the benefit. Excess alcohol and drugs not only dumb down the mind, they also harm the body.

When we learn to control the functions of the mind, we can easily reduce its interference and enhance its capabilities to gain a full perception in the present.

Wasteful Mental Chatter

> *"The biggest troublemaker you'll probably ever have to deal with watches you shave his face in the mirror every morning."*
>
> —Old farmer's adage

When you commit your psychic energy in the now, you get a clear immersion in the present. Not being present—even though you may be talking to your child or spouse—is the symptom of consciousness in the control of the mind. This kind of token involvement in the present suggests that you need to work on valuing other people so that you can dedicate your full attention to them.

There are so many distractions that your mind can create as you move from moment to moment. How many minutes of the day do we actually spend as undivided time with our loved ones in the present?

Clear perception is your loyal ally that will empower you in your journey toward success. When a person's vision is impaired by a cataract, their perception of the world becomes inaccurate. If you want to help that person, you must remove the cataract. Most people go through life with their perception of everything impaired by the mind. The untrained mind obscures and misdirects consciousness.

Arriving at Presence

If I were to give a graphic example of how it feels to roll back the chatter of the mind, I would say it is similar to how a pilot feels

8 / Principle 6: Being in the Present

when he crosses the sound barrier. When an aircraft approaches the speed of sound, the pilot can hear the roar of the engines, as well as the intense buffeting vibration of the aircraft as it penetrates the sonic build-up. Once the aircraft crosses the sound barrier, however, the pilot can no longer hear the engines because the sound is now behind the aircraft. The pilot sails smoothly through the air, without any sound of the engines or the intense buffeting. The diamond-like quietness is immediately perceivable. Similarly, when you quiet the chatter of the mind, perception becomes very clear and crisp. In this crystal clear state of mind, we experience full *sattva* and presence. It is like changing gears. We learn to move seamlessly from the mental platform to the clarity of presence.

Learning how to switch off the mind's chatter will bring you back into clarity.

Emotions are a good indicator of whether our mind is obstructing our vision or enhancing it. Therefore, we must practice observing our emotional state. When we are experiencing positive emotions such as joy, love, hope, determination and confidence, this is a sign that we are getting closer to our *sattva* state. This closeness to *sattva* broadens our psychic bandwidth which allows us to perceive life in the present.

When we observe negative emotions expanding, however, this is a sign that our perception is clouded by patterns of the mind. These patterns are the faulty beliefs and judgments our mind retains about ourselves and others. Some people believe the mind must always be churning out ideas. Remind yourself that without the interruption of the mind, you are a greater person.

Allowing the mind to steal our psychic energy and continuously burn it up by thinking on and on weakens the clarity of presence. We have to limit the amount of wasteful mental chatter the mind tends to produce.

By going deeper and getting in touch with our *sattva* state, the natural symptoms of our very self will arise. Those symptoms are permanent feelings of combined love, joy, peace, and a feeling of pure connection to everyone. Magnifying these positive feelings and remaining situated within them will bring us into presence consciousness.

Many people negatively judge themselves and subconsciously punish themselves with a set of faulty beliefs that limit their success and happiness. Therefore, it is imperative to move beyond the false "you" of the mind. Stop judging, forgive yourself and others, and remove the faulty patterns of thinking that restrict your efforts to develop mastery.

You exist now, so forget the past and future. Be here now and vibrate happiness and joy.

The deeper you turn inward, the steadier your daily base of happiness and peace will become. As you get in touch with yourself, you will begin to vibrate different levels of love toward others. The deeper you go, the more you will see the universal connection between yourself and others. This will cause you to vibrate a sweeter form of love toward everyone. When others feel those intense vibrations of care and affection, they will automatically want to reciprocate.

Constant mental chatter cuts off the fountain of peace, bliss and youthfulness which is at the core of being present.

8 / Principle 6: Being in the Present

Connecting to the Present

It is very important while interacting with others to realize that the mind will try to trick us to submit to its influence by any means. Therefore, we should understand that our ears are the pathways to circumvent the mind. By applying psychic energy to hearing what others are saying will help connect to them through your heart. Similarly experiencing clear eye contact or visual absorption will free us from the stress and resistance the mind imposes. Try to get in touch with your true senses by perceiving directly, and not through the mind.

The senses of the body are conduits that communicate with the real senses of the self in *sattva*. The wrongly patterned mind tries to color this sensual data with its interpretations and judgments. Attaining *sattva* or "presence," however, means to circumvent the mind through direct perception. The tools in this book and our seminars will help you learn how to empower direct perception with psychic capital and circumvent the negative patterning of the mind.

When we are resonating in sattva, *we will feel a strong, pure love for everyone.*

It is only when we speak from the heart that we can maintain this state. If we are not congruent with pure feelings, we have again surrendered to the mind. Don't allow the mind to control you from the background, for the mind will always try to find a way into your presence. The mind will try imposing a false persona or shadow self and its shadow values and attitudes to obstruct your unrestricted state of *sattva*. Therefore, always remain congruent or true to the feelings emanating from your inner self.

Harness the Mind with Intelligence

> *"Intelligence is quickness in seeing things as they are."*
> —George Santayana

> *"The test of first-rate intelligence is the ability to hold two opposed ideas at the same time, and still retain the ability to function."*
> —F. Scott Fitzgerald

You may be wondering if shutting off your mind means losing your intelligence—your sense of discrimination. The answer is that intelligence is actually situated beyond the mind. Therefore, *sattva* is a state in which we are observing with intelligence. Intelligence sees things as they are, whereas the mind tends to categorize things. With intelligence, we can try to understand an object's purpose. While observing people or animals in our *sattva* state, our intelligence can understand what they are feeling by their appearance and movements if we resonate with them. Therefore, intelligence actually becomes stronger without the distraction of the mind.

With intelligence, we can harness the function of the mind in positive ways. For instance, intelligence can instruct the mind to focus attention. Switching off the mind's constant chatter does not stop the cognitive aspect of self; rather, switching the mind off allows cognition to be accurate and true.

If you want to experience unlimited joy and powerful strength in your daily life then you have to begin by improving just one day. Since life is made up of days, a repeated endeavor to improve daily will make for a perfect and blissful life. By RASIC (Regulated And Steady Improvement Consistently), mentioned earlier, we can dis-

8 / Principle 6: Being in the Present

solve the false persona or shadow self that the mind has created. We can become situated in our true identity for success and feel unlimited happiness and joy. We can feel joy by interacting with others as we marvel at their beautiful existence.

Becoming solidly balanced in sattva *means that there will be no more doubt, feelings of unhappiness, failure, and loneliness; rather we will begin to enjoy the unlimited reservoir of happiness from within at every moment.*

Happiness—The Result of Being "Present"

> *"The gift of happiness belongs to those who unwrap it."*
> —Unknown

> *"You are never fully dressed without a smile."*
> —From Annie

Allow Yourself to Experience Inner Happiness

Material pleasure, although it gives us a temporary feeling of happiness, if it is not perceived correctly can also contribute to the duality of the mind. Therefore, we should not hanker for sensual pleasure but rather strive to unlock the unlimited bliss from within.

You must believe and understand that all joy and happiness comes from deep within you. Therefore, magnify your desire to attain freedom from the shackles of the mind and senses, and happiness will emanate from within automatically. There is no need to expend psychic energy by dwelling on sensual pleasure, for such dwelling only ensnares your consciousness on the mental plane.

Unlocking the Doors to Happiness

Begin to allow yourself to experience the internal happiness that is condensed and flows within you. You are the source of all your happiness. Stop allowing the mind to impose its unlimited conditions on your happiness. When you become happy because someone compliments you or makes you feel good, locate the internal source of those good feelings. Ask yourself: "Where did the order to release that happiness come from?" You will notice that the order came from a pattern in the mind, a small part of its rule book of criteria for releasing happiness. In deep thought or meditation, rewrite that pattern to say: "The source of unlimited happiness is from within and I will experience it at every moment."

Cessation of Pain or True Happiness?

Some people consider happiness to mean merely the cessation of misery. In feudal times, one of the punishments given to criminals was to tie them to a chair and then lower them into a river or lake from a bridge. The wrongdoer would be dunked underwater for a few minutes, and then lifted out as he or she gasped for breath. After just enough time had passed to inhale a lungful of air, they would be dunked into the water again.

By experiencing this for a few hours, accused criminals became used to the dunking in the water and it became their reality. Being brought up for air began to feel like pleasure. Because of the contrast between the drowning experience and the relief of getting air, they would see the gasping for breath as the greatest source of pleasure.

Is this the kind of pleasure we have become accustomed to? After the stress of the morning rush-hour commute, a tiring day in the office and then the evening bumper-to-bumper traffic on the freeway, relaxing at home in front of the TV may seem like

8 / Principle 6: Being in the Present

pure bliss. It is strange how relief from suffering can appear to be so blissful. When you find relief, like the criminal being brought up for air, it seems as if there is no higher state of happiness.

Through these commonplace examples, it is plain that appreciation for a pain-free existence may become amplified to the point where relief of suffering is seen as happiness. Although breathing is something we do all the time, we don't consider it a source of happiness until we experience prolonged suspension of breath.

Usually when we experience happiness, certain conditions are met whereby we decide that we can become happy. For instance, if we receive a bonus or increase at work, we become happy. Perhaps your son gets accepted into a prestigious university, and you have a feeling of pride and happiness. If someone pays you a compliment, you feel better about yourself and may even experience a flash of joy. During all of the above experiences, we unleash our joy because certain conditions have been met. When these conditions are met, we decide to award ourselves by feeling happy.

No one is giving you the happiness, however: the happiness comes from within yourself.

What causes us to experience this happiness only when certain conditions are met? Why don't we allow our joy to flow out all the time? Is there a limit to how long we can remain constantly happy? The first thing we should realize is that happiness is our original state: it is our true self which is the fountain of ever-flowing joy. Most of us can remember a time in our life when we were extremely happy, in fact totally blissful. Unless this bliss was inherent in ourselves, how could we experience it? How can we unleash happiness if it is not inside us already? The problem is that we hold a faulty belief that we need certain conditions to enjoy our inherent happiness.

> *"Plenty of people miss their share of happiness, not because they never found it, but because they didn't stop to enjoy it."*
> —W. Feather

> *"When one door of happiness closes, another opens; but often we look so long at the closed door we do not see the one which has been opened for us."*
> —Helen Keller

> *"Happiness is the delicate balance of what one is and what one has."*
> —F. H. Denison

Unconditional Happiness Blocked

The ancient *Vedas* say that we are *sat-cid-ananda*—our consciousness is eternally imbued with ananda or unlimited happiness. What causes us to cover these feelings of inner bliss and only unleash it under certain conditions? The answer is that we are reacting to a pattern in the mind of thinking that happiness is dependent on external conditions. This faulty belief has created a habit of switching our happiness on and off. This pattern is a driving force for the basic hunter-gatherer instinct of eating, sleeping, mating and defending necessary to sustain our body. Therefore, our consciousness becomes affected negatively when we don't do the activities it deems necessary for survival. This negative response is the shutting down of our inherent feeling of happiness.

When we satisfy these needs, the body triggers a hormonal response that makes us feel happy.

The Trap of Consumerism

Consumerism works because it tells us that advertisers' products enhance our survival. Advertising, combined with social pressure, convince us that consumer products are an essential part of the list of things necessary for survival. When we don't get these objects, we experience the shutting down of internal bliss. Allowing ourselves to be controlled by the pattern that ensures survival drives us to become entrapped by consumerism. Becoming a victim of these control mechanisms leaves people feeling devoid of happiness always, with huge internal pressure to acquire the products that are foisted on us. If people allow themselves to be controlled by a consumer-driven society, where new demands are created every day, true joy will be driven into hibernation.

In order for us to experience our inherent happy condition of life all the time, we must practice unleashing it unconditionally. The mind is the center of the software that drives and influences our perceptions and experiences. When experiencing our happiness, we need to restrict the influence of the mind and perceive reality and life directly. In other words: live in the now or get in the zone. As we get older, we tend to raise the bar higher and higher on the conditions needed to become happy. What made us happy as a child could have been as simple as climbing a tree or watching the birds in the sky. Now many complex expectations and demands drive us to work harder and harder to access our own inner reserves of pure joy.

By practicing sattva *or mental balance, we actively change the patterning of the mind to exhibit our inherent happiness unconditionally.*

Beliefs That Lock Out Happiness

We have to change the pattern or faulty beliefs that make us depend on external conditions to experience happiness and presence. Much of the stress and depression experienced in society is self-inflicted. When we remove our dependence on external conditions, we allow ourselves to be joyful all the time. Binding happiness to external conditions is a type of self-judgment. We bind ourselves to rules and conditions before we can enjoy our natural exuberance. Building up expectations is another way we punish ourselves. For instance, we may tell ourselves that "If the Yankees win the game, I will feel blissful all day." In this way, we connect happiness to an outcome that is completely out of our control.

When we are pleasantly surprised, complimented, praised or rewarded, we feel happiness spontaneously, because we suddenly feel good about ourselves. If our self-esteem is boosted, we reward ourselves with happiness. We have positioned a judge to stand at the storehouse of our happiness, rationing out joy according to his book of false beliefs. What if you could feel good about yourself all the time? By practicing *sattva*, the psychic capital you build up will nurture your self-esteem, confidence, perseverance and many other positive emotions. By increasing these emotions and by challenging your faulty beliefs, happiness will begin to shine out of your being and affect everyone around you.

The Law of Diminishing Returns

One of the qualities of real happiness is that it endures. Most of us confuse pleasure with happiness. When we feel pleasure, we

8 / Principle 6: Being in the Present

award ourselves with some happiness. Pleasure is a good sensual feeling that lasts for some time, but depends on sensual stimulus. By repeating a particular physical pleasure continually without interruption, the senses begin to supply diminutive returns of pleasure. For example, if you keep on eating ice cream, you will get brain-freeze, and after sometime you will feel ill. Soon the sight of ice cream will make you nauseous! Because the body has limits and sensual pleasure is linked to the body, we must conclude that sensual pleasure itself is also limited.

If we link our happiness directly to sensual pleasure, we sign ourselves up for a roller coaster ride on which we must experience the peaks and valleys of sensual pleasure and pain. The unique quality of internal happiness, whether we call it spiritual happiness or the happiness of consciousness, is that it is not limited by the senses and increases as consciousness blossoms in *sattva*.

Happiness is a state of consciousness that comes from within, and therefore is a phenomenon that can be increased and made to endure.

See happiness as your natural state not dependent on outside criteria. The first step towards increasing your happiness is to distinguish happiness from pleasure. Begin to see how happiness is a state or underlying emotion of consciousness. Then challenge and break down the false beliefs that restrict your flow of happiness. If someone is nasty to you, why feel bad and punish yourself by depriving yourself from your natural state of inner joy? Instead retain your happiness within yourself and feel compassion for those who take pleasure in being nasty to others.

Don't allow others to control your flow of happiness. Don't judge yourself by others' attitudes toward you, but rather be committed to constantly improving your inner exuberance and contentment. By making a commitment to happiness, others will automatically feel happy in your company, and even try to learn to become like you.

Pleasure and Pain Come of Their Own Accord

If we accept pleasure and pain when it comes of its own accord, and not let it modulate our inner state of joy, we can experience consistent and increasing happiness. Pleasure is a necessary part of life, as it accompanies eating, resting, listening to music, sex and many other activities. Pain is also an inevitable part of our lives. In fact, the human body has more nerves that deliver pain than pleasure. Who hasn't smashed a small toe against a bedpost or door and felt the excruciating pain our bodies are able to deliver? Pain, like pleasure, is unavoidable.

Three sources of pleasure and pain:
    1) From other people
    2) From the environment (such as inclement weather)
    3) From our own bodies and minds (in the form of disease or imbalance)

Maintaining your happiness equilibrium during pain may seem difficult, but with practice you can master it. As a contrast, genuine happiness comes directly and inherently from you, the person, not from your mind or your body. Happiness is as inherent to us as sweetness is to sugar or heat is to fire. Happiness is our consistent nature, and as such has the ability to increase more and more.

Seven suggestions to get in touch with your inherent happiness:
    1) Smile as often as possible.
    2) Tell yourself that you deserve to be happy unconditionally.

3) Ask yourself everyday: "What can I do to improve my state of happiness?" (Not pleasure)

4) Try to make others happy by smiling, complimenting, and taking an interest in them.

5) Find any excuse to laugh. Laughing condenses and stimulates our happiness.

6) Challenge false beliefs that restrict your happiness.

7) Don't allow the influence of the environment, your own body, or other people to shut off your inner bliss.

Summary of Steps to Uncovering Your Internal Happiness

1) Understand that diversionary activities are a temporary measure to circumvent the mind, and that part of a more permanent method is to learn to ignore the mind.

2) Learn to access true happiness through "optimal experiences" that are congruent with your purpose.

3) Become aware that the rule book for receiving happiness is linked to our hunter-gatherer instinct and should be rewritten to allow unconditional access to happiness.

4) Learn how to remove the stress of conditional rules and tap directly into your happiness.

5) Be aware of the massive effort of our consumer society to entrap you in the hankering and lamenting process by linking their products and services to an essential need triggering an instinctive hunter-gatherer response for happiness.

6) Material senses will deliver both pleasure and pain. Sensual pleasure has a diminishing return and pain although temporary is unavoidable.

7) Maintain a connection to your inherent happiness by becoming balanced in *sattva* consciousness and elevating your center of awareness above the mind.

A Quick Recap

- High risk, extreme behavior—sports, intoxication, etc.—are attempts to fulfill the need to participate in life with the highest amount of attention. Heightened perception is a desirable platform from which to perceive reality, but these activities yield temporary results and in most circumstances come with a high price tag.
- Optimal experience, or "being in the zone," and the accompanying happiness, can be experienced perpetually by learning to control the mind and focusing one's psychic energy on our life's purpose and the task at hand.
- To reach the higher stage of *sattva*, a person has to elevate his consciousness beyond the intellect and direct it deep into the heart. It is through the opening of the lotus petals of the heart, currently protecting our real consciousness within, that we genuinely connect with our innermost self, which is imbued with pure love, absolute, full *sattva*, and true knowledge. This is the secret of being in the present.
- Emotions are a good indicator of whether our mind is obstructing our vision or enhancing it. Therefore, we must practice observing our emotional state. When we experience positive emotions such as joy, love, hope, determination, and confidence, it is a sign that we are getting closer to our *sattva* state. This closeness to *sattva* broadens our psychic bandwidth which allows us to perceive life in the present.
- To experience unlimited joy and powerful strength in your daily life, start by improving just one day. Since life is made up of days, a repeated endeavor to improve daily will make for a perfect and blissful life.
- True happiness is inherent, not just the cessation of pain and distress.

8 / Principle 6: Being in the Present

- Unconditional happiness can be blocked by faulty beliefs created by the mind and external influences like the lure of consumerism. It is different than ordinary pleasure which is affected by the law of diminishing returns.
- Both pleasure and pain come of their own accord from three sources: our own mind and body, others, and the environment. Real happiness is beyond this duality.
- Follow the seven suggestions listed to get in touch with your inherent happiness.

CHAPTER 9

Principle 7: Sattva Mastery

"I am the master of my fate; I am the captain of my soul."
—William Ernest Henley

"Life is change. Growth is optional. Choose wisely."
—Karen Kaiser Clark

"To make your dreams come true, you have to stay awake."
—Unknown

The First Step to Living the Life of Your Dreams

IF YOU'RE THE KIND of person who strives to experience complete freedom and a healthy and happy life, then this chapter will resonate with you. Understanding your purpose is the first step to living the life of your dreams. The next step is to move confidently in that direction. This is the key to a life of mastery.

Like a competent captain sailing your ship on the ocean of life, you understand that knowledge of your location, setting the right course, and maintaining that course are all equally important factors for reaching the destination.

In the fast-paced world in which we live, it is very tempting to do whatever is necessary to pay the bills, and subsequently bury your dreams and desires. What most people discover is that by the time they return to digging up their dreams and their inherent purpose in life, they are already set in their ways and frightened to change.

If you want a life filled with wonderful journeys and adventures, the key to your happiness and success is to always strive for mastery.

The pursuit of mastery is an endeavor to get closer to the true nature of self. Connecting with your purpose brings you closer to mastery and to being "in the zone." With confidence that you can realize meaning in your life, you must be willing to focus your energy on achieving mastery.

The result of mastery is that we feel great about ourselves and enjoy the process of getting there.

If you are asking fundamental questions such as "What do I believe in?" and "What lifestyle do I really want for myself and family?", then you are striving toward the real, internal, meaningful side of you. This drive advances us to a higher state of consciousness as humans. Some call this state self-realization, *nirvana* or perfection.

The *Vedas* talk about the perfection of your state of mind as leading to unlimited joy or *ananda*. This perfected state of mind the *Vedas* describe, is the state of striving for mastery and balance within yourself. When there is no internal conflict between your activities and purpose, there is a chance that you can easily achieve mastery. Being free from conflict will increase your psychic capital and fuel your happiness, confidence, compassion, and magnetism so you can achieve mastery and success.

What Is Mastery?

The question may be asked: "Can anyone pursue mastery?" The answer is that mastery is the fulfillment and perfection of our inherent dreams, desires, meaning and purpose, and is therefore everyone's real self-interest.

No matter what your occupation is, you can derive great satisfaction by becoming absorbed in the mastery of your work within your chosen vocation in life.

Enjoying the Pursuit of Mastery

Self-realization that emphasizes leaving aside duties to family and society is impractical. We can see that all the great philosophers have talked about a middle way, a path of self-mastery within the domain of normal life. This is the true meeting of science and religion, and of work and renunciation. Mastery of self brings ultimate happiness and success within all spheres of life. But we must truly aspire to mastery in order to set ourselves on a path to actualizing our divine, inherent gifts.

It is not that we must strive to reach the end or goal, the zenith of perfection or become the best in the world at something. Instead, why not enjoy the process and pursuit of mastery? A recreational sailor does not strive to reach the next port when he knows that several airlines can take him to his destination much faster, but he nevertheless enjoys the process of sailing.

It is mastery of the process of life that we must learn to enjoy, and not reaching the road signs along the way.

When we overcome obstacles and succeed in our endeavors, we naturally feel happiness and confidence. Although there may be difficulties on the path of mastery, those very same difficulties become the pillars of strength and the fuel of motivation to succeed. With each hurdle overcome, we feel a sense of self-purification and lightness.

As discussed in previous chapters, the *Vedas* call *dharma* the idea of centering ourselves on our purpose and meaning. Acting according to our *dharma* is considered an elevated state of consciousness that delivers success while allowing us to remain balanced. Pursuing the fruits of success without understanding purpose or *dharma* will ultimately end in dissatisfaction.

Real success can never be achieved when we bury our purpose and meaning to life deep within ourselves.

Type B and Type M Persons

There are two types of people: those who believe they are limited to their present intelligence, situation, lot in life and sphere of experience, and those who do not feel bound to their present or to their past. The first type of person doesn't generally strive for mastery of self, but instead is motivated by things he or she wants. I call those who limit themselves Type B persons: B for Bound to Bodily Limitations. They are not advancing toward their purpose, but rather prefer to chase after external objects.

The second type of person believes there is no limit to how much they can learn, achieve, experience and expand their consciousness. They are motivated by strong beliefs and a search for meaning, and want to benefit others by their actions. These type of people gravitate toward mastery and I call them Type M persons. Here M stands for Mastery, Maturity and Motivation.

Society, the media, and even our educational systems emphasize and encourage Type B consciousness. People with Type B drive, are easier to steer and control. The old-school workplace where workers have to clock-in and clock-out tends to suppress people into a Type B mentality where their value is measured in hours and minutes.

In the new and improved workplace, people are treated according to their inherent abilities and their contribution. This kind of environment encourages vocational thinking and Type M personalities. Therefore successful companies have found that facilitating Type M people with more latitude, flextime and respect for their value and contributions yields greater results than purchasing people's time.

Type M people tend to work harder when they are driven by internal motivations, whereas Type B people work as little as they can get away with, and have to be prodded by carrot-and-stick motivations. By the export of their jobs to places like China and India, and the influx of cheap labor through their borders, Americans have been forced to move toward innovation and Taaaype M workplaces. As business and society demonstrate more awareness of the science of mastery, there will be a paradigm shift in the workplace and industry toward encouraging Type M consciousness. Research and studies in positive psychology give ample proof that businesses and people following Type M strategies yield success more frequently.

Unlike Type B persons who ignore or deny their purpose, Type M persons live for their purpose in life. Many people have buried their inner purpose so deep within their consciousness that they have already forgotten why they are unhappy. Plagued by feelings of depression, emptiness and low self-esteem, they take refuge in intoxication and indulgences for temporary relief. An awakening of meaning and purpose can immediately overcome all negative feelings. When you strive for purpose, your consciousness becomes optimized to its natural human capacity. Anything less than centering your life on your purpose will deprive you of your humanity and happiness.

The Culture of Steady Improvement

> *"The only place success comes before work is in the dictionary."*
> —Satchell Paige

> *"People don't change because they see the light.
> They change because they feel the heat."*
> —Unknown

One of the main aims of this book and our workshops is to point out the benefits of adopting a culture of steady improvement on a constant basis. This improvement has to be tempered with balance so that it can endure and nurture happiness. Improvement without balance is destined for failure.

Balance without improvement results in mental calcification. Flexibility, balance and improvement together generate success and happiness.

Even though we may be in *sattva*, "in the zone" or experiencing flow, additional desires will nevertheless always enter the heart. The process of enlightenment does not mean the termination of all desires; rather it means to follow desires that are congruent with our purpose and our heart. Becoming expert at identifying real desires that stem from the heart, and ignoring those that originate from outside influences, will help you pursue desires that are

9 / Principle 7: Sattva Mastery

most beneficial for yourself, and those in your sphere of influence. *Sattva* allows us to act and interact in a balanced and effective way.

Sattva *helps us get more done while feeling happier and making others blissful in the process.*

Attaining this peak state empowers us with the tools to accomplish more or influence many people in a positive, dynamic way. In this connection it is important for us to analyze our desires. One of the first questions to ask ourselves is whether a desire is an internal one, stemming from the heart, or an external one, arising from the mind.

External desires are desires that originate outside of the self, defined as a quantitative activity such as going on a cruise, buying a new car, investing in a home or climbing Mount Everest. These kinds of desires can be explicitly articulated having a specific beginning and an end. These kinds of desires goad one to obtain the fruit or the end result of activities. Frequently external desires are within the realm of things money can buy.

On the other hand, internal desires are defined qualitatively, and are focused on things that money can't buy, such as becoming compassionate, influential and charitable, spending more time with friends and family, enhancing relationships with the ones you love, doing exercise on a daily basis, making a commitment to be honest, preparing for marriage, or practicing attentive communication.

External or explicitly defined desires usually involve the mere acquisition of an object which requires planning, determination and focus to achieve. These kinds of desires may add temporary joy to your life, create lovely memories and perhaps enrich you as a person. Internal desires, however, result in permanent internal changes to one's routine habits, behavior and emotional patterns, such as a counter-productive attitude that we would like to change. These desires are powerful, life changing glimpses into our true nature. We may want to transform the way we see ourselves or others around us, or increase our level of physical health by swimming or doing yoga and pilates daily. Internal desires include empowering our state and magnifying our emotions so that we can change our behavior, perception and attitude. Dynamic, internal desires change who we are, as well as the way in which people perceive us.

Transforming Your Emotional State

> *"Flaming enthusiasm, backed up by horse sense and persistence, is the quality that most frequently makes for success."*
> —Dale Carnegie

What Distinguishes Successful People from the Rest?
Successful people are like giants with magnified personalities. To be successful, you too must learn to control and empower your emotional state. Emotions are powerful tools, the cue cards for intensifying consistent happiness. Magnifying your emotional state influences people around you in positive or negative ways. When we magnify our negative emotions, we exert a damaging effect on our children, loved ones and anyone around us. On the other hand, when we magnify our positive emotions, we influence the people around us in uplifting and inspiring ways. Those who magnify their positive emotions intensify their own and others' happiness and success.

What Is the Secret to Becoming a Magnetic Influence on Others?
The secret lies in the power to invest psychic capital to fuel

our positive emotions. This entire book discusses techniques to conserve our psychic capital through balance in order to magnify positivity. If we don't conserve psychic capital, the stamina needed to empower our emotions cannot be properly fueled. Through consistent steadiness and balance in our activities and consciousness, we can build up our psychic reserve. The key to success is utilizing this reserve in positive ways. If you have to deliver a presentation to the board of directors of your company, how will you impress them with a confident, vibrant, powerhouse of magnetic exuberance? Practicing mastery over your emotional state allows you to influence others.

Where Does Inspiration Come from?

Inspiration comes when people see your vision and feel the intensity of your emotional commitment to that vision. This intensity of emotional commitment convinces others that you have firm confidence to achieve your goals. Since everyone wants to be on the winning team, being decisive, determined, enthusiastic and convincing will effortlessly attract others to connect with your vision in a powerful way. Abraham Lincoln once said: "Always bear in mind that your own resolution to succeed is more important than any other." To attain this state of mind, we have to believe in what we are setting out to achieve.

Once you have decided to pursue your real identity or dharma, *belief and conviction in your goals becomes second nature.*

Empower Your Emotional State

Conviction, belief, and determination are great, but greater still is when we empower these states of mind.

There are four stages from conception to action, which are:

> Thinking
> Feeling
> Willing
> Acting

It is the feeling that drives you to willing and acting. To succeed, you must empower your emotional state to energize your actions toward success. By energizing your actions, a higher resolution of life is experienced and consistent happiness is felt through such "live action."

When you don't empower your actions with emotions, they become weak and less effective.

To become expert at empowering emotions, you need to get in touch with them first. If you find yourself moving from one hour to the next unable to feel enthusiastic, do something to change your state of mind. It may be exercise, or listening to a motivational speaker, putting in extra time with someone you love, or listening to your favorite music. Begin to observe your emotional state regularly. Make a sincere effort to magnify the emotion that is needed to get peak performance for the activity at hand.

This process can be likened to putting your foot on the fuel pedal in a car, as it will give you the power you need to focus dedicated attention, resulting in a higher resolution of experience.

This higher resolution of experience is a deep feeling of satisfaction in activity, being "in the zone" or being "in flow." As you empower your emotional state with your psychic capital, you will become happier and influential. You will begin to enjoy all your activities and find happiness in the process of being successful.

9 / Principle 7: Sattva Mastery

Feeling happiness in the process of success is the key to moving forward, since happiness expands your psychic capital.

By consistently practicing to improve your emotional state, you will become sensitive to how you invest your psychic capital. When you see the effects of allowing others to anger you, you will become very concerned not to allow this. In fact, you will become so protective of your valuable and powerful psychic reserve that you will never allow the thieves of anger, stress, and depression to rob you of it again.

Identify the emotions you want to empower. For instance, when you spend time with your family, are you empowering the emotions that will nurture them with love and confidence in themselves? When learning something from your teacher or mentor, are you showing great inquisitiveness, enthusiasm and thankfulness for his or her time and effort? When dealing with your business associates, are you empowering your vision with emotions of enthusiasm, determination, and confidence? When planning your own day, are you investing the emotional capital needed to ensure you will consistently improve the quality of the tasks you set out to do?

Using the RASIC technique, discussed in an earlier section, work on empowering your emotions throughout your day. Avoid feeding the negative emotions. If you suddenly find yourself consumed by a negative emotion like anger, envy or depression, do something to change your state. By calling or visiting a good friend and empowering your friendship with them, the negative emotions will go away. Don't allow negative emotions to claim any permanent place in your mind. By diminishing their influence, you will become healthier, wealthier and wiser.

Max Linder on Influencing Others

A scene from a silent movie with Max Linder demonstrates how powerfully your emotional state can affect others. In this film, Max is dancing in a ballroom with many high-class socialites. Everyone is dressed fabulously, and the men are all wearing tuxedos with bowties and tails. During the dancing, the other guests notice that Max's tails are torn a little. After a while, Max notices that people are laughing at him, so he goes to the restroom. After looking in the mirror, he notices that his tails are torn a little up the middle. Max grabs hold of the two tails and tears them all the way up to the collar. He then goes back into the ballroom and begins to dance flamboyantly, his tails flying around as he swings here and there with his partner. With his enthusiastic smile and dance movements he becomes the center of attraction. Inspired, all the men begin to tear their tails all the way up to the collar and start dancing with the same gusto.

This is a wonderful example of how an emotional state can affect and influence others.

Begin to see your emotional state as a tool to fuel your happiness and success and the happiness and success of those around you.

Build Your Will Power

> *"Strength does not come from physical capacity.*
> *It comes from an indomitable will."*
> —Mahatma Gandhi

You can generate an enthusiastic longing and desire to achieve the results of action by building up your will power. Will power is built up by constantly focusing on the goal and the fruits thereof,

9 / Principle 7: Sattva Mastery

as well as determination to overcome the pain aspect of the activity to achieve the goal. Focus on the consequence of not pursuing your goals because not pursuing worthwhile goals always has painful consequences. All activity has a certain amount of pain associated with it. These words ring out true in the ancient wisdom of the *Bhagavad Gita* 18.48, where Krishna says, "Every endeavor is covered by some fault, just as fire is covered by smoke. Therefore one should not give up the work born of his nature, even if such work is full of fault."

Engaging the mind in focusing is good, but we must get it to focus on the reason why we want to pursue our goals, rather than the reasons not to pursue them.

Once having reached the willing and acting stage of attaining your goal, you must become fully committed to your course of action. This is where most people lose traction and either become distracted or unable to muster the emotional commitment to continue. To stay on the path of success you need to take control of your mind and become enthusiastic by reminding yourself constantly of the reasons why you decided to commit to an action.

Sometimes if the direction we have taken is not working, we have to become flexible and think of another way to achieve the goals we wish to pursue. Responsibility, commitment, and determination are all words that show a desire to overcome the short-term difficulties for the long-term reward. As the saying goes, 'God helps those who help themselves'.

If we make the commitment, we will earn the reward.

Empower Your Decisions

Another way to give strength to your decisions is to associate them with other powerful decisions which you made in the past that had a positive effect. Even if the mind tries to focus on the attendant difficulties, learn how to actively ignore the mind's tendency to sway you from your commitment. The more you ignore the mind's chatter, the sooner you will realize that these difficulties are no longer a threat to your survival. Once the mind becomes trained in this way, it will give up its resistance and free up the psychic energy it has been using to nag you. This psychic energy can then be used to feed determination instead.

Generating Enthusiasm

> *"Enthusiasm is the highest paid quality on earth."*
> —Frank Bettger

> *"No person who is enthusiastic about his work has anything to fear from life."*
> —Sammuel Goldwyn

Another effective strategy to generate enthusiasm is to maintain a list of all the commitments on which you followed through, together with your feelings at achieving the rewards of those goals. This list functions as your own personal score card. We should challenge ourselves to take on more commitments toward our regular daily improvement.

Key elements towards empowering our emotional state:
    1) Ask yourself, how can I achieve my destiny and success?
    2) Put a plan into action.

3) Focus on, and explicitly magnify, the positive reasons you need to follow your plan.

4) Ignore the mind's reminders of the pain associated with that endeavor. Instead, think of the pain incurred by not following through.

5) Associate your decision with other positive decisions you made in the past that were successful.

6) Commit all your psychic energy to feed determination to fulfill your commitments.

7) Remind yourself how you felt when you followed through on your commitments.

8) Constantly empower appropriate emotions through congruency and focus.

Consciousness and the Power of Focus

Sometimes people try intensely to stop their mental chatter by sheer concentration, but to get "into the zone," one must first relax the mind and let perception flow through.

Sattva, or being "in the zone," comes by quieting the mind. In traditional meditation, slowing the rhythm of breathing makes the mind automatically relax. At an advanced stage, one can relax the mind at will. Having flexible adaptive "core beliefs" (principles by which you live your life) produces relaxed consciousness. When the mind follows adaptive beliefs it has less resistance and empowers presence. Happiness flows with ease because the mind is relaxed. Having flexible core beliefs doesn't mean that one is willing to compromise one's moral and ethical values, it means that we become less judgmental of ourselves and others.

Calming the mind will automatically increase your store of psychic capital, thus fueling your determination and enthusiasm to happily pursue your success.

Music is another way to soothe and calm the mind in order to bring you to a state of balance and internal happiness. It is good practice to spend time daily listening to music and relaxing the mind. Maybe you like to meditate in a quiet place or relax in a hot bath. Whichever way works for you, find the time to center in peace to observe the perfection of life. Practice maintaining this adaptive state longer and longer. Eventually with practice, you will experience a constant feeling of internal happiness and an abundance of energy.

Learning how to use this energy is your key to success. The energy of consciousness should be channeled into fueling your positive emotions and activities. Don't allow negativity or scattered mental chatter to rob you of this valuable resource. By entering this state of focused consciousness, consistent happiness will accompany you. The key to unlocking human potential lies in the secrets of consciousness.

That blissful contentment is not from any type of bodily pleasure but rather a permanent underlying state of happiness that is part of the very core of your existence and being.

Harnessing the Power of Focus

The power of focus can be compared to a muscle that we flex to turn off the chatter of the mind. By focusing, we are telling the mind that we don't want distractions. Like a muscle, the power of focus may be difficult to exercise in the beginning but later it becomes easy! In the past, meditation and yoga were used as a

9 / Principle 7: Sattva Mastery

method for putting one in the zone. These methods are still very useful when we know what the objective is and can see the benefit of the results.

By practicing to use your focus power, what you are really doing is:
   1) Restricting the influence of the mind.
   2) Zooming in on a particular perception.

These two activities require practice. Like a photographer who closes one eye to look through the lens with the other, we switch off the analytical side of our mind to perceive with the artistic or feminine side of the mind. Just as a photographer may use either a wide angle lens to capture a football stadium or a macro lens to focus on the spots on a butterfly wing, similarly with perception unclouded by the mind, we can choose to perceive the whole scenario or focus in on any particular aspect of it.

The process is to turn down the volume of the mind's chatter, and then decide what to focus on, allowing us to experience a higher resolution of interaction.

Focus for Peak Performance

When one becomes steadily situated in *sattva*, focus becomes sharper and clearer. In this state our store of psychic capital now primarily nurtures positive emotions such as confidence, determination, hope and enthusiasm, and thus increases.

Concentration is the ability to commit full consciousness toward a particular subject. Light is so powerful that it can dissipate darkness. When light is focused and concentrated it creates a laser, a ray of light so dense that it can even penetrate metal. Consciousness is like concentrated light. We concentrate psychic energy either when we want to learn something, or when we want to perform an action. For instance, we may concentrate our minds in order to spot a person we know who is arriving at an airport, or we may concentrate similarly when learning to fly a helicopter for the first time. Concentration can be seen as an active dynamic interacting continually with our perception, whereas focus can be described as a "being there," in-the-now observation of our perception.

In order to be successful and in peak performance, we must learn how to focus and concentrate through practice. Such practice will automatically switch off the chatter of the mind. We must also learn how to direct focus while reducing mental chatter. The benefit of "being in the zone," or not allowing our focus to be broken by branching out our psychic energy on many things at once, is the blossoming within of positive emotions such as determination, perseverance, compassion, love and happiness, which in turn fuel our psychic capital.

To succeed we must be able to follow RASIC: Regulated And Steady Improvement Consistently. It is through determination, hope, and consistency that we can improve ourselves constantly. When our improvement is constant, not being hampered or distracted by the mind, success is near. Our determination to control the mind must be sure. To achieve success, determination and flexibility are the key states to maintain. To remain determined and flexible, we must see clearly, within our mind's eye, the benefit and the outcome of our endeavors. If we want to become financially independent, physically healthy, free from stress and depression or to find the partner of our dreams, we must become determined to practice *sattva*—and be flexible in altering any calcified faulty beliefs we still harbor.

9 / Principle 7: Sattva Mastery

In sattva, *we establish the balance between our desire for success and our current situation through mental agility and emotional flexibility.*

Practice withdrawing the mental chatter and preconceptions of the conditioned mind until you master it. Developing mastery over your mind will help you achieve the greatest success and happiness you deserve. Once mind mastery is achieved, you will learn how to empower yourself further by unleashing positive emotions at will. By practice, you will become free from the interference of the mind. Eventually, as consciousness develops, you will be able to access your awareness beyond the limitations of mind and faulty inclusions within the intelligence.

Selective Perception

An optimal experience is induced when consciousness becomes focused and undivided. Picture a child lying in a cradle on a peaceful spring morning. The sky is azure blue. Above the cradle, an oak tree spreads its gnarled branches. The baby is absorbed in the sound of the breeze playing through the trees. A small fountain nearby makes a cool, splashing noise as the water cascades into the pond below. Birds are chirping playfully. The child is smiling as he absorbs the beauty of nature and perceives all the sounds, smells, sights and sensations on his skin. This richness and depth of absorption invokes within the child a feeling of happiness. Just by being present, he feels happy. Many of us have experienced this heightened quality of perception while involved in our chosen vocations.

With a mind that is not yet conditioned, the child is free to commit all of his consciousness without the interference of a distracted mind. By observing in this way, the child naturally has psychic clarity. One of the reasons that children learn as quickly as they do is due to their ability to make use of all of their bandwidth to absorb reality and learn from it. The mind of the child is learning what it should accept or reject, what causes happiness or distress, and who is a friend or foe. The child's mind begins to recognize patterns and generate rules as to what ought to be focused on and remembered.

As we get older, our minds become conditioned to certain patterns of thinking, and therefore they automatically discard increasing amounts of information. The selective perception of the mind acts to protect and nourish the growing child, a type of auto-pilot function. For adults who haven't yet learned how to switch this selective filter on and off, it grays out or covers their clear perception of reality and the world around them. Consequently perception is channeled and colored according to our conditioning and selective attention.

What other obstacles add to this conditioning of the mind? Television and other media persuade us that we can only be happy if we obtain their advertisers' products. We pay attention to media and advertising that push us toward desiring their products, even if only on a subliminal level. People's minds are being trained and consistently influenced by advertisers, educators and societal norms to link happiness with external pleasure. Most people unconsciously see television as authoritative and as a source of valid information. As the parable of the king's new clothes suggests, if an authoritative source tells us that an object or particular worldview will make us happy, we believe them.

Without a conscious endeavor to find purpose in our lives, we become controlled by the media and the overall motivations that drive our economy.

9 / Principle 7: Sattva Mastery

Due to the phenomenon of targeted and bombarded advertising, our selective perception is programmed to distract us from our real source of happiness. We hanker for things we have grown to believe will make us happy but in actuality only give us temporary amusement.

This book and our seminars teach you how to switch off the auto-pilot that keeps your life on the mediocre level, as well as how to remove the patterns of thinking that obstruct greater depth and resolution of your perception. It will help you to regain control of your psychic energy and build up its valuable psychic capital. We'll give you the tools to take command of your most powerful faculty—the mind.

By switching off mental chatter you can engage the mind in what it does best: pure focus and unadulterated concentration!

The Three Waves in the Ocean of Emotions

> *"We can't stop the waves, but we can learn to surf."*
> —Jonathan Kabat-Zinn

Even when you feel you're in a balanced and peaceful state of mind, you may notice that your consciousness can be drastically affected by 1) your body, 2) others, 3) your environment. These external influences affect your internal balance at a subtle level, and can disturb your mind-stream unless you learn how to cope with them.

Besides influences mentioned above, there are three very powerful subtle external influences that compete to control you. These are like three frequencies that take control of your mind and influence it. Almost like a weather forecast these three influences have their prominence over you at different times. You can however learn how to transcend their influence by learning how to switch off the mind that is directly affected by their influence.

These influences can be likened to waves, which are classified in the Vedas *as:*
    1) *Tamas* (withdrawal and selfishness)
    2) *Rajas* (very active, intensity without much thought)
    3) *Sattva* (balance and illumination)

The ideal mood of your mind-stream is *sattva* (balanced). Maintaining the mood of *sattva* requires keeping your psychic energy centered and balanced.

Understanding the Waves of Life to Unlock Their Power

Like a mariner on the ocean of life, we have to navigate our way around dangerous waves. *Rajasic* or intense waves toss and turn the consciousness of a person frantic to move ahead with many poorly devised plans. These waves create stress and anxiety and eventually wear down stamina and confidence.

    The worst kinds of waves are *tamasic,* which thrash at you with such great force that you become disorientated, and lose direction and purpose. These *tamasic* waves can throw you down into an ocean of depression and misery.

The good news is that sattvic waves of energy are beneficial and push you toward your purpose. The sattvic waves can be likened to a favorable wind in the sails, as they breed great confidence and happiness.

These three types of subtle energy waves are always present in life, and therefore you may be affected by their influence, no matter how confident and successful you are. The key to success is to recognize these waves for what they are, and then to harness the energy of these influences without being negatively affected by them. Realizing that the world is not within your control will help you to accept that such influences will come and go just as the seasons come and go. The central principle is to be prepared to act proactively in such circumstances.

Tamas

The wave of *tamas* or withdrawal makes one more prone to laziness, depression and lack of self-esteem with no goals. At night, the influence of *tamas* should be utilized to assist in sleep. Since the wave of withdrawal has more influence at night, people tend to get more involved in activities of that mode, such as going to nightclubs, or getting intoxicated. This mode influences one to withdraw from meaningful activities and gravitate toward selfish indulgences. Used positively it can be harnessed for relaxation and even meditation.

Rajas

The *rajasic* wave is a flowing force field of nature that prompts passionate activity. We can see the influence of this wave during the rush-hour traffic, when everyone is scurrying around frantically to get to or from work. Picture a busy shopping mall on the day before Christmas, with crowds of shoppers rushing around trying to buy gifts for their loved ones. This is one example of people working under the mode of intensity.

Being influenced by this wave of intensity, one tries to accomplish many things one after the other without thinking of the consequences of the endeavor, or who might be disturbed in the process. In the mode of intensity, people act with much energy but without much thought. A person afflicted by waves of intensity will experience a lot of stress and anxiety. A person in the mode of intensity can't sit still for very long and is always running around. Foods that fuel the mode of intensity include things like deep-fried, spicy, hot and over-cooked preparations.

Sattva

In the mode of balance or goodness, one is motivated to maintain a healthy body and a clear mind-stream. The mode of goodness or *sattva* influences us to act correctly according to our purpose. If we compare these three emotional drives to the construction, maintenance and demolition of a building, *sattva* or goodness is equivalent to the maintenance, intensity to the construction and withdrawal to the demolition.

The external forces of *sattva* or goodness and balance inspire us to do good things. Taking care of your health, getting up early in the morning, and keeping your environment clean are all desires prompted by *sattva*. Certain environments are more conducive for the influence of goodness and balance. For instance, a sunny, quiet garden on a spring morning is conducive to inspiring *sattva* or goodness, whereas a dark, noisy nightclub evokes a tendency toward indulgences and ignorance.

Keenly observe the influence of these waves and their effect on your psychic energy. If you allow yourself to be influenced by the waves of *tamas* and *rajas*, your psychic energy will be burnt up by either stress or anxiety.

The wave of sattva *empowers your psychic capital and enhances your personality and purpose. Therefore nurturing* sattva *or goodness is always beneficial because it puts you in balance.*

9 / Principle 7: Sattva Mastery

Riding the Right Wave

Unlike your internal state of mind which you can control, the external world is out of your control. Therefore mastery of the mind means to keep the mind unaffected even while in proximity to the negative waves of *rajas* and *tamas* (intensity and withdrawal). It could be a matter of keeping your cool while in rush-hour traffic or remaining sober while others intoxicate themselves. Peer pressure and mass hysteria are similar instances of powerful external pressure to act in ways in which most people normally would not. Therefore, it is a good idea to think before you act or react. You can practice this skill by silently counting to ten if you're being provoked by these external waves of passion or ignorance, and then try to center yourself in the peace of *sattva*.

Mastery is the ability to always remain in control of your mind and actions. Mastery is the drive to work toward your meaning and purpose in life without being dragged away by waves or influences that are working against that purpose.

Overcoming these external influences may be hard work at times, but by doing so you will become stronger and more purpose-driven. Like a trained mariner, you will become expert at using these waves to assist and remind you of your purpose. When you become more familiar with the influences of these waves, you will be able to harness their energy to thrust you toward your purpose. All of these influences when properly harnessed can assist you toward achieving your goals.

The energies of nature can be rough and devastating, but the same energies can assist and empower you. Like a scalpel in the hand of a trained surgeon, what is potentially very dangerous can become beneficial. Living in the now will make you more aware of the changes and influences that are presenting themselves. By identifying and recognizing these external influences, you will be able to maintain your internal mental balance. You will conserve your psychic energy and empower your positive state of mind. Real happiness can be achieved by overcoming the influences of these outside forces.

Balance can only be found when you gain control of your psychic energy, unleash your internal happiness and learn to remain steady, even though battering storms of endless combinations of these waves. Sometimes known as biorhythms that tend to swing our mood, these waves when properly harnessed can become a force to drive your true purpose.

Remaining steady does not mean that you lose feeling or sensitivity, but rather that you see things as they are, and repose your energy and emotions in a way that gives meaning to your life and the lives of others.

Seeing things as they are means that you learn to use the energy of these modes of nature in the proper way so that they become favorable to your progress. Like a martial artist who uses the weight of his opponent's attack against the opponent, we can unleash the usefulness in all these energies when we master the art of recognizing and manipulating them.

One of the most powerful ways to attain mastery is to learn how to "zoom-out" to see the big picture. Become broad-minded, in the *Vedas* the term *mahatma* means broad-minded and the term *duratma* means narrow-minded. So the key is to learn how to unrestrict your consciousness and zoom out or see the bigger picture.

9 / Principle 7: Sattva Mastery

A Quick Recap

- Feelings of success or failure are felt within in direct response to the setting of your internal purpose-driven compass that prompts you toward your true goal. Self-mastery is when there is no internal conflict between your activities and purpose, the mind becomes peaceful and your psychic capital increases.
- Whether you are a Type B or Type M person was revealed to you.
- One of the main aims of this book is to point out the benefits of adopting a culture of steady improvement on a constant basis. Improvement without balance is a long walk to success. However, flexibility, balance, and improvement, when combined, generate success and happiness quickly.
- To be successful, learn to control and empower your emotional state. Emotions are powerful tools, the cue cards for intensifying consistent happiness and peak performance. You learned the eight key elements to empower your emotional state.
- The two ways to increase your power of focus is by resisting the influence of the mind, and by zooming in on a particular perception.
- The three waves, or influences of nature (ignorance, passion, and goodness), were described in detail. The best wave to ride for a successful life is *sattva* (goodness).

CHAPTER 10

Sattva and Faith

IN THE PROCESS of attaining self-mastery, most of us will exert considerable effort in challenging faulty beliefs that are obstructing our inherent happiness. During this process of ever-expanding transformation, we will naturally encounter questions of spirituality and religion.

While engaging with the process of internal reprogramming, some may feel that religion and faith are areas where they would rather not tread. After all, faith or religion is a very personal choice. There are many religions in the world which appear to recommend similar teachings. Although religions are comparable in terms of teachings, their essential differences are often found in their understandings of the identity of God and how to worship Him. The goal of this book is to help improve ourselves. Let us not forget that God helps those who help themselves.

In today's world it is very easy with tools such as the internet for anyone to find out mountains of knowledge about all the different religions and faiths. Religion, when properly understood, can vastly improve our desire to elevate our consciousness. With the widespread practice of yoga, *kirtan* and mantra meditation much of the Eastern traditions of faith have been absorbed into our Western culture. In the East the culture of the West has become all pervasive. The key is to adopt the best of both Worlds, like the blind man carrying the lame man on his shoulders. God, by definition, must be an awesome loving God who becomes pleased when His creation lives in harmony, peace and love.

Self-Improvement in Wisdom Literature

Whether one chooses to accept the idea of God or not, the concept of self-improvement is a universally accepted practice. Here are some quotations that urge self-improvement from a variety of religious texts which you may find helpful:

"Do not conform any longer to the pattern of this world, but be transformed by the renewing of your mind." (*Holy Bible,* Romans 12:2)

"You were taught, with regard to your former way of life, to put off your old self, which is being corrupted by its deceitful desires; to be made new in the attitude of your minds; and to put on the new self, created to be like God in true righteousness and holiness." (*Holy Bible,* Ephesians 4:22–24)

"The most important aspect of the process of self-improvement is the cultivation of one's sense of humility before the Creator. This, however, should not be an artificial undertaking, but a goal of one's efforts. If, as a result of working on the self, an individual gradually starts to develop this quality, then it means that he is proceeding in the right direction." (*Talmud, Avodah Zarah*)[16]

---

[16] Quoted in a commentary on the *Kabbalah* by Rabbi Michael Laitman, *Attaining the Worlds Beyond: A Guide to Spiritual Discovery* (Ontario, Canada: Laitman *Kabbalah,* 2003), p. 444.

10 / Sattva and Faith

"An individual need not despair when, as he studies and works on improving himself in an effort to attain spiritual elevation, he comes to see himself as being in an even worse condition than prior to studying *Kabbalah*. The true nature of egoism is revealed to a person whose level is higher than that of others, and for this reason a person becomes worse in his own eyes, even though he has actually become better." (*Talmud, Megillah*)[17]

Although a non-theistic path, Buddhism teaches a method of self-improvement with the Noble Eightfold Path—right understanding; right purpose; right speech; right conduct; right livelihood; right effort; right mindfulness; and right perception.

We send our children to school to help them improve their lives and future. Governments fund social welfare programs to upgrade the lives of their citizens. Countries of the world arrange international meetings to reduce global warming and emissions, with the goal of improving life on the planet. Therefore, the notion of upgrading humanity individually and collectively has always been a universally accepted ideal.

There are three areas of improvement that most religions of the world address in depth:

1) Individual—improving yourself personally.

2) Interactive—improving how you interact with the world and others.

3) Universal—improving how you interact with God and/or the universe.

I am of the opinion that by striving for improvement in at least the first two categories, we can vastly enhance our personal expe-

---

[17] Laitman, *Attaining the Worlds Beyond*, p. 446.

rience and the experience of others in this world. This is not to say that we must neglect the notion of improving our concept of God or the absence of God, but rather that the first two categories represent common ground. It is this common ground that is a vast area of human existence and interaction, an area that desperately needs a pragmatic paradigm shift, a universal upgrade of consciousness.

As humanity stands between a drive for destruction and the need for conservation, personal choices can shift the critical mass in the direction of positive change.

By upgrading our existence individually and interactively, we enter into a heightened state of existence. We begin to experience life in higher resolution and release the happiness within. Some may ask: "How does the *sattva* state affect a God-seeking person?" The answer is that *sattva* adds greater vibrancy and a higher definition to all experiences. If you are a person of faith, *sattva* prepares you by cleansing the heart and focusing your love and devotion toward the Lord. If you believe in the peace of nirvana, *sattva* unlocks within you the balance of a Zen Master, the compassion of Mother Theresa and the steadiness of the North Star.

Therefore, whether you consider yourself a Christian, Muslim, Jew, Hindu, Buddhist or atheist, Sattva will undoubtedly enhance your experience.

Improvement Begins from the Core

We start by upgrading ourselves individually. By reprogramming the faulty thinking that causes us pain, suffering, doubt, fear, anger and hopelessness, we begin to transform our lives and achieve the enormous reward of happiness, success, love, satisfaction, peace and hope. By upgrading through *sattva* interactively, our relationships and perception of others will flourish. We will no longer be affected by negative people, even when they consider us enemies.

Upgrading our consciousness is our birthright and one of the fundamental purposes of human life. Individual upgrade is the first step to improving the future of our children and the planet. By improving ourselves and our interaction with others, we become the instruments for the much needed change our planet deserves. *Sattva* will enhance your personal experience of life to such an extent that you will want others to experience this colossal transformation. Just as we should expect great things from ourselves, we should also have great expectations for others.

Look Within First

We live in a society of freedom of speech where many people are strongly opinionated and unafraid of voicing their beliefs. So it is important to be tolerant of others beliefs as part of our correct perception in *sattva*. The transforming or upgrading of consciousness will improve the character and faith of any religious or non-religious person. Therefore, to allow your consciousness to blossom and bloom will be the greatest investment of your life. Those who criticize others' faiths, without questioning their own faulty conceptions risk falling into the trap of becoming fanatics and radicals. This brings to mind the words of Jesus in John 8.7: "Let those without sin caste the first stone."

Why look at others' stock of faults when we possess a warehouse of faults within? It is only this burdensome warehouse of faults that deprives people of their real purpose and mastery— their real happiness and peace.

Becoming successful, happy and peaceful begins with the transformation of our own mind and heart. You may think that by somehow earning more money, or by changing your spouse's attitude, or by attaining a better car or house you will become satisfied. This is the greatest illusion, that something external and material will enhance your experience of life.

This attitude is like thinking that by merely driving a car with mechanical problems into an uptown neighborhood, the problem will be automatically resolved. This sort of thinking is absurd. We need to slow down, become attentive, and repair any faulty thinking that is obstructing us from achieving happiness and success.

A Quick Recap

- During this process of ever-expanding transformation, we will naturally encounter questions of religion and faith. It is not that we need to dispute our faith: rather, by improving our selves, we improve our faith.
- Whether one chooses to accept the idea of God or not, the concept of self-improvement is a universally accepted practice. Whether you consider yourself a Christian, Muslim, Jew, Hindu, Buddhist, or atheist, *sattva* will undoubtedly enhance your experience.

CHAPTER 11

Balancing a Society On the Verge of Change

WHAT IS THE IMPORTANCE of collective human enlightenment? How does humanity upgrade consciousness to engender progress in universal empathy and transcendent mental clarity? How do we, as a group, tap into internal joy and personal mastery? Humanity goes through different trends or cycles. These cycles are driven by what becomes the priority of the people. In the Vedas there are four drives; *dharma*—religiosity, *artha*—economic development, *kama*—sensual pleasure and *moksha*—liberation from mundane life. When society is driven by religiosity the churches or religious institutes dictate the rules and lifestyle. A society driven by economic development emphasizes production, mechanization and materialism. When sensual enjoyment motivates a society then all endeavors, legislation and governance encourage and protect individuals' rites to enjoy their senses in whatever way they choose. Emphasis on elevation of consciousness signifies a society that values spirituality and the eternality of the soul. When we look back on the last few centuries we can see how these different cycles become prominent from time to time. By zooming out we can move from improving ourselves to elevating society as a whole.

Most of us have been taught that the age of human progress and enlightenment began in the early Renaissance period and matured during the Enlightenment Era. During this period of widespread change, a downgrade of individual perception, veneration, confidence and faith in the world's monarchies, colonialists and clerical bodies, lead to universal social unrest and a transformation in society for the "better." The new world brought industrialization, education, modernization, scientific and medical progress. The reduction of religious and feudalistic dependence fostered, in turn, an era of autonomy, reason, secularism and egalitarianism. We have seen a similar effect of collective dissatisfaction toward dictatorships taking place in the beginning of 2011 in the Middle East and North Africa.

Mounting Dissatisfaction

Phases of mass dissatisfaction have reoccurred in society since the dawn of civilization. What are the forces that drive universal dissatisfaction, and in whose hands should the fulfillment of this drive lie? The core ideals that germinated from the Enlightenment reflect two premises: the need to transfer the mechanism of responsibility for governance of our society from corrupt leadership to the people; and a redirecting of social, economic and political goals to encompass individual autonomy, equality, justice for all and freedom of belief and speech. These steps began to open the path for humanity to pursue freely and openly a life on a higher level.

A review of the history of the twentieth century reveals great progress in the attainment of the first premise, namely the transferring of the governance—from monarchies, colonialists, the institutionalized church, superstition, tyrants and oppressors—to a

11 / Balancing a Society on the Verge of Change

form of democracy in some places, and quarantined, monitored Banana Republics in others.

A collective frustration is bubbling up in human society that is invigorating the other ideals of the Enlightenment movement— the establishment and facilitation of individual autonomy, equality, justice for all and freedom of belief and speech.

That premise challenges economic, political and civil goals to encompass humankind's fundamental higher drive. This higher drive is the prime formula to improving the networks that make up our societies.

Even though the lifestyle of an average modern family rivals that of the Royal families in previous centuries, there is still mounting dissatisfaction with the way things are. Great strides in social sciences have revealed deep problems with the economic system that delivers our sophisticated and modern lifestyle. There is a collective global shift in how people want to be treated by governments and corporations, prompting a dire need for such institutions to reevaluate their objectives and the way they treat people.

After wrestling the reins of power and control from corrupt dictatorships and bishops, we have largely succeeded—at least in the Western world—in placing the control and power in the hands of the people, who have unfortunately then ceded control to corrupt corporations, politicians, lobbyists, and interest groups. However, even though life may not be perfect, it is a lot better than what it was before.

But although we find ourselves living more sophisticated lifestyles, the average person feels just as powerless and oppressed as he or she did under the feet of colonialists, autocrats and theocrats.

Two hundred and fifty years of freedom have passed, but have we succeeded in satisfying the underlying reasons for dissatisfaction? Do we find ourselves failing to gain clarity on the higher needs of human society? What drives our happiness, compassion and contentment? Is the pursuit of our higher selves counterproductive to the industrial freight train that we have empowered?

To be clear, let us look at what drives human happiness and contentment:

1) The initial hunter-gatherer drive for eating, sleeping, mating and defending.

2) The collective social, political economic drive.

3) The aspiration toward a higher spirituality an inner happiness.

The Enlightenment movement has fared well in competently addressing the first two categories of human drives, but falls short on satisfying the third drive toward spiritual wellbeing and inner happiness. This third drive requires the nurturing of the connection between humanity and the metaphysical or divinity.

Another reason that the upgrade of consciousness to a transcendent or spiritual level has been neglected is the culturally dominant view that this area is both vitally personal and reserved primarily for the clergy of different faiths. Clergy of all religions have duped us to believe that we are therefore totally dependent on them for inner happiness or a transcendent upgrade.

If humanity is to take charge of our collective and individual enlightenment program, it will most likely occur when mounting dissatisfaction in that sphere reaches a critical mass. Much collective scientific research has been undertaken to explore this most important aspect of human nature. Even though a wealth of recent social science research exists, most governments have

11 / Balancing a Society on the Verge of Change

not embarked on programs to restructure society according to the conclusions that this research has offered. The main reason for this neglect is that governments themselves are still operating according to old models of apathy and resistance to change. Until the level of dissatisfaction breaks through the envelope of our collective tolerance, nothing will change globally.

Striving for Idealism

As people become dissatisfied with the unbalanced mainstream culture, they turn to alternate cultures, often replicating history and older civilizations where the same process took place. The human cultural landscape tends to move from emphasis on materialism to a striving for idealism and mysticism.

For instance, between 1815 and 1848, Europeans became rebellious and dissatisfied with the Enlightenment's structured, impersonal and mechanistic way of life. Due to their (sometimes misdirected) efforts, a counter-Enlightenment took place that matured into the Romantic movement. The Romantic revolt was inspired by a vision of idealism, the arts, mysticism and anti-rationalism. The hippie culture of the mid-1960s is a modern counterculture, defined by its anti-establishment drive—to reject everything that materialism stands for. Countercultures have existed in Western history as far back as the Ancient Greeks.

A danger exists when civilizations swing toward countercultures not tempered by thought, retrospect and empathy. Upwardly motivated tyrants sometimes elevate themselves upon this wave of change to fulfill their own personal agendas. Thus, failed countercultures breed violent movements such as the Christian Crusades, the Nazi movement in Germany during the twentieth century, and Islamic Fundamentalist terrorist organizations today. Most of the leaders of these movements desire to push their agenda on others by force. They will use any violent means possible to scare people into compliance. Fortunately, such movements are eventually rejected by society as they contradict our higher understanding of what it means to be human.

The Balance of Wisdom and Compassion

The solution to the unsettling political dialectic from one extreme to the next lies in properly addressing human needs from all perspectives. When we understand what is important not just for the flesh but also for the spirit, we can collectively forge a future that brings about universal human happiness with compassionate sensitive societies. By encouraging the teaching and practice of ethical values, empathy, deep contemplation, mental control, moderation, preservation of the environment and compassion to all the species of life, can we begin to satisfy our sometimes dormant—but always present—desire for spiritual enlightenment.

Empathy and Wisdom

In Tibetan Buddhism, the above symbol of the *srivatsa* (knot) represents the mutual dependence of religious doctrine and secular affairs, or the union of wisdom and method through the intertwining of knowledge and compassion. According to this system of theology, at the time of spiritual enlightenment, there is a dependent co-arising of the union of wisdom (*prajna*) and compassion (*karuna*). This elegant upgrade to human consciousness is the key to peace and happiness. The solution to this age-old dichotomy, offered by Tibetan Buddhism, finds a strong resonance in the philosophical work *Novum Oranamum*, by Sir Francis Bacon:

"Man, by the fall, lost at once his state of innocence and his empire over creation, both of which can be partially recovered even in this life, the first by religion and faith, the second by the arts and sciences."

This timeless need for the ongoing balancing of society finds eloquent expression in the writings of great thinkers throughout time. In the East, Buddha called it the Middle Way. Aristotle called it the Mean between the deficit and the extreme. Hegel called it Synthesis. The *Vedas* call it *sattva*. By practicing moderation, flexibility and compassion, humanity will rise to a standard of being that satisfies all our needs. By centering our consciousness and controlling our minds, individually and collectively, society will become balanced and happier.

In his book *Drive*, Daniel Pink calls the software that drives this new and improved society Motivation 3.0. A new culture of consciousness calls for greater individual autonomy, purpose and mastery. Pink supplies page after page of scientific proof which suggest that we perform better and live happier lives by offering our personal contributions, rather than selling ourselves as a commodity. Pink's opinions resonate strongly with evidence found in Viktor Frankl's *Man's Search for Meaning*,[18] which affirms that when we find meaning to our lives, we discover peace and happiness. When individuals attain a level of *sattva*, this upgrade brings a higher definition and deeper satisfaction to life as evidenced also in Csikszentmihalyi's book, *Flow*.

An upgraded social, economic and political system is not a negation of the present model but rather a synthesis that incorporates human needs, both material and spiritual.

---

[18] Viktor Frankl, *Man's Search for Meaning*, (New York, NY: Washington Square, 1985).

All the evidence points to the fact that we have spent far too much time changing our environment, circumstances and lifestyle, and hardly any time changing ourselves from the inside and transforming society to accommodate those changes. This book hopes to equip individuals with effective tools that can help satisfy their collective need for individual purpose, a higher resolution of happiness, a cultural atmosphere of mastery and deeper, meaningful relationships. Through adaptive changes to the way we think, we can upgrade our consciousness fearlessly and cross the threshold toward a richer, more meaningful way of life.

A Quick Recap

- Human beings have struggled for centuries with their march toward material progress, independence, happiness, and a way to elevate their experience and existence.
- Scholars have deliberated over what triggers such universal social, economic, and political change. When growing dissatisfaction reaches critical levels, this dissatisfaction becomes a catalyst to change.
- If change is not balanced with facilitating the inner needs of individuals, and is just creating better material facilities, then such change will be inadequate and result in more mounting dissatisfaction.
- This chapter examines both the benefits and the failings of the recent changes in society and discusses the need to balance the internal spiritual nature of people with the social, economic, and political needs and freedoms, to upgrade society to a higher level.

CONCLUSION

What's Next?

IN THIS BOOK I introduced you to the seven principles of *sattva*, universal principles that will bring balance, clarity, prosperity, and happiness into your life.

Briefly they are: Improving your health through diet, exercise and mindfulness is a daily practice that should be incorporated into your lifestyle and become second nature. Understanding and following your true purpose should become the goal of your endeavors and the impetus to the enthusiasm of your life. By bringing love into the center of all your relationships and becoming attentive to others, you will learn how to treat people the way you would want them to treat you. Learning how to remove all of the internal impediments that limit your potential will help you grow the gentle giant within and reveal you to be a person of stature. As you expand your consciousness, the secret of nature's abundance will become clear by the abundant blessings in your life. You will become at home in the present where you can engage in deeply satisfying activities in mastery. By this mastery you will offer the world, and those you love, a part of you. These tools will allow you to become the driver of your destiny and not just a frightened passenger. I hope you will take advantage of these powerful principles to guide you on your journey.

Our acceptance that change is beneficial for us is one of the pivotal realizations that move us to upgrade our life.

Positive change has two aspects: the knowing or understanding aspect, where we realize that change will help us improve our life, and the more difficult acting or doing aspect where we adapt our actions to become congruent with this higher understanding.

It is the action part of the process where most people get stuck. There are many reasons for this reluctance or resistance to change, but one of the most important obstacles to overcome is fear of failure and reluctance to try. It is by practice that we generate neural pathways that give us the confidence to adapt to a new lifestyle or activity. Therefore, a daily commitment to upgrading our activities and thoughts will empower dynamic change in our life.

The seminars and workshops we offer are an immersion program to begin building those neural pathways, and create a segue to transforming your life in a practical way. With the energy that fuels consciousness and the understanding of *sattva*, a person who improves their life with these seven principles will experience a higher level of vibrancy of life and learn how to develop mastery in their purpose.

Life is the most riveting interactive program there is, and learning how to achieve the most out of this journey will become the greatest reward.

Please visit my website at www.sattvalife.com to discover more resources to help you on your journey.

Glossary

Alankar—Ornamented expression of a particular *raga*, or musical scale.

Ananda—Unlimited bliss or happiness inherent in consciousness

Artha—Vedic term for economic development; the second stage in a sequence of events that leads to successful human existence

Beingness—psychic clarity, an altered state of unusual depth and lucidity

Bhakti—pragmatism fused with devotion, purpose and service to God; also used to denote pure, unalloyed love of God

Bhakti-rasa—the drive for relationships that stems out of pure love

Buddhism—ancient Eastern philosophy based on the teachings of Gautama Buddha, the aim of which is to transcend the cycle of birth, suffering and death

Chit—knowledge

Citta-vrittis—Vedic term for mental patterns

Dharma—Vedic term for an individual's inborn life purpose; the first stage in a sequence of events that leads to successful human existence; an understanding of what constitutes the essential nature of all things; also refers to the observance of moral standards and ethical values

Jnanakanda—idealism, organicism, and renunciation

Kama—Vedic term for sense enjoyment; the third stage in a sequence of events that leads to successful human existence

Karmakanda—materialistic pursuits

Karuna—Vedic term for compassion

Middle Way—path of moderation between the extremes of unlimited sensual indulgence and harsh self-denial recommended by Buddhism

Moksha—Vedic term for spiritual enlightenment; liberation from the cycle of birth and death; the fourth stage in a sequence of events that leads to successful human existence

Nirvana—Sanskrit term for blissful union with the Supreme after liberation from the cycle of birth and death; a joyful state of freedom from encasement in a physical body, from greed, anger and delusion; the goal of self-realization, perfection of life

Prajna—Vedic term for wisdom

Pranayama—breathing meditation

Psychic bandwidth—the complete spectrum of mental energy available to an individual, the potential of which many of us have not realized yet

Glossary

Raga—specific musical scale according to the system of ancient Indian music

Rajas—category of universal energy or mode of nature which embodies the qualities of passion, according to the *Vedas*

Rasa—specific mood or set of emotions

RASIC—Regulated And Steady Improvement Consistently

Sat—eternality

Sat-cid-ananda-vigraha—Vedic term for the inherent nature of consciousness; literally translated as "eternal form, full of knowledge and bliss"

Sattva—category of universal energy or mode of nature which embodies the qualities of goodness, according to the *Vedas*

Srivatsa—Tibetan Buddhist symbol denoting an endless knot; it represents the mutual dependence of religious doctrine and secular affairs, or the union of wisdom and method through the intertwining of knowledge and compassion

Surya Namaskara—sequence of classic yoga postures recommended in Vedic literature for attaining optimal health; literally translated as "salute to the sun"

Swami—one who has attained self-mastery, the name for a spiritually-centered person in Vedic literature

Tamas—category of universal energy or mode of nature which embodies the qualities of ignorance, according to the *Vedas*

Type B Person—someone who is Bound to Bodily Limitations; he or she is not advancing toward his or her purpose, but rather prefers to chase after external objects and people

Type M Person—someone who is Mature, Mellowed, and gravitates towards Mastery; he or she is motivated by strong beliefs and a search for meaning, and want to benefit others by their actions

Vigraha—purpose-shaped form; according to the *Vedas*, the eternal, spiritual form all souls are meant to possess

Wah—traditional Japanese term for harmony in social relationships and domestic surroundings

List of Works Cited

Csikszentmihalyi, Mihaly. *Flow: The Psychology of Optimal Experience.* New York, NY: HarperCollins. 1990.

Edelman, Sarah. *Change Your Thinking: Overcome Stress, Anxiety, and Depression, and Improve Your Life with CBT.* Cambridge, MA: Da Capo. 2007.

Frankl, Viktor. *Man's Search for Meaning.* 1985 ed. New York, NY: Washington Square. 1946.

Kegan, Robert and Lisa Laskow Lahey. *Immunity to Change: How to Overcome It and Unlock the Potential in Yourself and Your Organization.* Boston, MA: Harvard Business. 2009.

Laitman, Rabbi Michael. *Attaining the Worlds Beyond: A Guide to Spiritual Discovery.* 2nd ed. Ontario, Canada: Laitman Kabbalah. 2003.

Patanjali. 2300 BCE. *The Yoga Sutras of Patanjali.* Interpreted by Mukunda Stiles. New York, NY: Weiser. 2001.

Pink, Daniel. *Drive: The Surprising Truth About What Motivates Us.* New York, NY: Riverhead. 2009.

Prabhupada, His Divine Grace A. C. Bhaktivedanta Swami. *Bhagavad-gita As It Is.* Bangalore, India: India Heritage Foundation. 1972.

Prabhupada, His Divine Grace A. C. Bhaktivedanta Swami. *The Nectar of Devotion: The Complete Science of Bhakti-Yoga.* A summary study of Srila Rupa Gosvami's *Bhakti Rasamrta Sindhu.* London, UK: Bhativedanta Book Trust. 1972.

Sinek, Simon. *Start with Why: How Great Leaders Inspire Everyone to Take Action.* New York, NY: Portfolio. 2009.